# Establishing Workplace Integrity

Dear Edward

Our entire family was so sorry
to hear about Judy's Passing.

You are all in our Prayers.

Best wishes

Paul
4/7/24

# Establishing Workplace Integrity

## Six Lessons in Values-Based Leadership

Paul Fiorelli, JD, MBA

BUSINESS EXPERT PRESS

Leader in applied, concise business books

*Establishing Workplace Integrity: Six Lessons in Values-Based Leadership*

The cover image is entitled "Discovering Your Inner Ethics", concept by Toria Wheelright—2017 Cintas Graduate Ethics Fellow, with design and fabrication by Jeff Norgord.  Used with permission by Xavier University

Cover design by Aaftab Sheikh

Interior design by Exeter Premedia Services Private Ltd., Chennai, India

First published in 2024 by
Business Expert Press, LLC
222 East 46th Street, New York, NY 10017
www.businessexpertpress.com

ISBN-13: 978-1-63742-581-7 (paperback)
ISBN-13: 978-1-63742-582-4 (e-book)

Business Expert Press Business Ethics and Corporate Citizenship Collection

First edition: 2024

10 9 8 7 6 5 4 3 2 1

*Alla Famiglia (to the family)—from "Moonstruck"*

*Much love to Libby, Katie, Brian, Stephie, Joe, Liz, Caleb,*
*Willem, Vivian, Loli, Ada, Linda and my parents Ralph and Gloria.*
*You all inspire me to follow the West Point Cadet prayer of choosing*
*the harder right over the easier wrong.*

# Description

A strong business case can be made for the value in values for business leaders. Companies like FTX, Theranos, Enron, and Worldcom crashed and burned when their founders used fraud, deceit, and corruption to obtain short-term goals and stock price spikes. Values-based leaders (a.k.a. VBLs and principled principals) like John Pepper (former CEO of Procter & Gamble), Jim Burke (former CEO of Johnson and Johnson), and Michael Woodford (former CEO of Olympus) had their personal ethics compliment their company's values to deal with potential business crises.

This book explores values-based leadership in different settings and perspectives, including the leader, employees, and the organization. The lessons focus on the themes of:

- Corporate culture;
- Employee loyalty and engagement;
- Motivations for improper behavior;
- Going inside the mind of a whistleblower;
- Crime and punishment for organizations;
- White-collar crime for individuals.

It is written in a practical voice, sprinkled with business case studies and pop-culture references from movies, songs, and TV shows and follows the life cycle of work, mostly from a U.S. outlook. Several chapters contain an Appendix for interested readers who'd like a deeper dive into a topic.

Each lesson starts out with an overview of the main concepts covered. These act as Executive Summaries or teaser outlines. Each summary will be followed by the main event, and the chapters include the historical background of the topics, progressing to the present day.

## Keywords

values-based leadership; corporate culture; employee loyalty; employee engagement; fraud triangle; whistleblower; compliance program; white-collar crime

# Contents

# Testimonials

*"I found Paul Fiorelli's book totally fabulous! I don't normally get excited about reading professional works as I am focused on learning and internalizing the materials like cramming for an exam. After the first couple of pages, I was totally absorbed in the book. It was by no means a cramming for an exam read. It was immersion in a great story with a need to banish everything that might take me away from it. The mix of pop culture with teaching principles keeps the text light while emphasizing important concepts. The various anecdotes and details included took on a thriller vibe and positively drove home the points and purpose of the work."*—**Molly Akin, Assistant Vice President Corporate Compliance, Constellation Insurance**

*"Professor Paul Fiorelli provides pragmatic advice on how to build an ethical culture in any organization through story-telling and real-life examples. This book is as entertaining as it is insightful and inspiring. A must read for those who want to grow values-based leadership in themselves and their organizations."*—**Martha Sarra, Vice President and Chief Ethics and Compliance Officer, The Kroger Co**

*"As the founder of a financial services compliance consultancy, I see the impact that ethics and integrity have on the success of investment advisers every day. Likewise, I see that firms that ignore ethics find themselves without clients or success very soon.*

*The anecdotes and guidance that Professor Fiorelli shares in his new book are simple to understand, quickly able to be emulated, and most importantly, will have a direct positive impact on any business leader or employee looking to improve the culture of their organization."*—**Matthew A. Swendiman, CPA, Chief Executive Officer, Key Bridge Compliance, LLC**

# Foreword

I first met Paul Fiorelli in January 2013 when he asked me to come to the Cintas Institute for Business Ethics at Xavier University to talk to his students about exposing the fraud at Olympus and how my comfortable life as a CEO of a multinational corporation suddenly spiraled out of control. I have spoken at leading universities around the world, including Harvard and Oxford, together with numerous corporations and other institutions. However, Paul made the greatest impact of any host in that he has such a pure interest as to what motivates human misdemeanors, and his curiosity always comes through the students he has taught.

In this book, through his six lessons, Paul explores areas few have attempted in such a practical way and provides insights that are valuable to anyone with an interest in corporate governance. He has a particular sensitivity in conveying the isolation and fear many of those who have blown the whistle feel at the time and are forever haunted by their experience.

When you read the coming pages, you will learn much about integrity and leadership, but to me, the most important lesson is the universal frailties of human nature and how all of us are susceptible to crossing the line between right and wrong.

Paul Fiorelli makes clear the responsibility upon us all to support those who want to do the right thing to get the truth out when the odds are stacked against the individual from the very beginning.

**—Michael Woodford, MBE**
Former CEO of the Olympus Corporation and patron
of the UK whistleblowing charity, Protect

# Acknowledgments

I'd like to thank my colleagues who took time out of their schedules to review this book and make valuable suggestions—Kristy Grant-Hart, Pat Gnazzo, Jeff Belle, Molly Aiken, Matt Swendiman, Martha Sarra, and my wife Liz Haradon. Special appreciation goes out to Michael Woodford for his encouragement and friendship and for writing the book foreword.

Thanks to Xavier University, Dr. Rachel Chrastil, Katherine Miefert, Michael Josephson, Ken Patel, Aaftab Sheikh, Jeff Norgord, and Toria Wheelright for permission to share parts of their stories in this book.

Thanks to the publishing team at Business Expert Press including Scott Isenberg, Michael Edmondson, and Charlene Kronstedt along with the team at Kriyadocs (Exeter Premedia) for their patience and expert editing.

Finally, I'd like to thank all my students over 40 plus years of teaching at Xavier University for their willingness to explore the importance of being values-based leaders.

# Prologue

## What Is Values-Based Leadership, and Why Should We Care?

### Introduction

"History has demonstrated repeatedly that leaders that lack ethical and values based dimensions can have serious adverse consequences on their followers, their organizations, our nation and the world," —Mary Kay Copeland.[1] We've seen this dire prediction carried out by value-less leaders over the past decades. Whether it is Sam Bankman-Fried (FTX—2020s), Elizabeth Holmes (Theranos—2010s), Bernie Madoff (2000s), the unholy trinity of Ken Lay, Jeff Skilling, and Andy Fastow (Enron—1990s), or Ivan Boesky (1980s), each one represents a failure of values-based leadership. The fact that they all ran their companies into the ground renews our interest in the value of values and leading with integrity. Values-based leaders (also referred to as VBLs or principled principals) apply their ethical standards to the business and seek like-minded employees to join them. These virtues include self-reflection, balance, humility, authenticity, integrity, and trust.

#### Self-Reflection

VBLs need to carve time out of their busy schedules to think about and evaluate how they will lead. What are their strengths and weaknesses? Once identified, can they be improved? Did they do what they said they were planning on doing that day, and if not, can they explain why not? Are there any lessons they can learn from these changes so they may do things differently in the future?

### Balance and Humility

Does the values-based leader consider other perspectives? If so, do they incorporate these into their decision making? The humble leader believes they can gain valuable insight from team members. On the opposite end of the leadership spectrum, others take a more egotistic approach and manage with an iron fist. The message from these bosses to their followers is clear—"It's my way, or the highway."

### Authenticity and Integrity

Leaders can talk about values, but the rest of the organization needs to see congruency between words and deeds. They need to be aware of Ralph Waldo Emerson's 1875 quote—"What you do speaks so loudly, I cannot hear what you are saying." Do associates believe these principals will lead with the principles of transparency, consistency, and integrity? Acting honorably isn't situational. It becomes a habit based on repeated good deeds, not just when it is convenient or public, but all the time. Charles Marshall is quoted as saying "Integrity is doing the right thing, even when no one is watching."

### Trust

The 1960s torch song singer—Etta James—sang, "Trust in me, in all you do. Have the faith I have in you." Warren Buffett had similar thoughts about that principle—"Trust is like the air we breathe—when its present, nobody really notices; when its absent, everybody notices." Trust acts as both a noun (the thing we give) and a verb (the act of giving it). The trusting party ("Trustor") must be willing to be vulnerable, giving their faith to another ("Trustee"). According to researchers Mayer, Davis, and Schoorman, the Trustor must believe the Trustee has the capacity to perform the act requested (ability), will act on their behalf (benevolence), and behave ethically (integrity).[2]

Trust is iterative. During the initial dealings with a new Trustee, Trustors make the leap of faith that the Trustee will carry out their duties faithfully. Consistently acting with integrity builds this trust. If the previous transactions went well, Trustors gain more confidence in dealing with the Trustee in the future. However, trust can be challenging to maintain and easy to lose. In a 2014 USA Today article former Under Armour CEO—Kevin Plank—discussed how trust is built in drops but lost in buckets.

An April 2023 poll by Gallup reported, "only 21 percent of U.S. employees strongly agree that they trust the leadership of their organization."[3] This percentage increases dramatically to 95 percent when employees emphatically believe three things happen. Trusted leaders:

- Communicate clearly;
- Inspire confidence in the future; and
- Lead and support change.

A 2021 report from Deloitte makes an excellent business case about the importance of trust.[4] Its findings include:

- Trustworthy companies outperform untrustworthy companies by 2.5 times.
- 88 percent of customers who trust a company bought from that company again.
- 79 percent of employees who highly trust their companies feel motivated to work.
- 94 percent of global boards believe in the importance of building trust for their company's performance.
- 85 percent of CEOs believe trust is critical for employee motivation.

## Case Study P.1—Procter & Gamble's Purpose, Values, and Principles

Many companies talk about the value of their values. In 1987, future Procter & Gamble (P&G) CEO—John Pepper—led the process to develop and memorialize the company's Purpose, Values, and Principles (PVPs).

### *Purpose, Values and Principles*[5]

Taken together, our Purpose, Values and Principles are the foundation for P&G's unique culture. Throughout our history of more than 180 years, our business has grown and changed while these elements have endured—and will continue to be passed down to generations of P&G people to come.

Our Purpose unifies us in a common cause to improve more consumers' lives in small but meaningful ways each day. It inspires P&G people to make a positive contribution every day. Our Values reflect the behaviors that shape the tone of how we work with each other and with our partners. And Our Principles articulate our unique approach to conducting work every day.

### *Our Purpose*

We will provide branded products and services of superior quality and value that improve the lives of the world's consumers, now and for generations to come. As a result, consumers will reward us with leadership sales, profit and value creation, allowing our people, our shareholders and the communities in which we live and work to prosper.

### *Our Values*

#### Integrity

We always try to do the right thing.

We are honest and straightforward with each other.

We operate within the letter and spirit of the law.

We uphold the values and principles of P&G
    in every action and decision.

We are data-based and intellectually honest in advocating
    proposals, including recognizing risks.

### Leadership

We are all leaders in our area of responsibility, with a
deep commitment to delivering leadership results.

We have a clear vision of where we are going.

We focus our resources to achieve leadership objectives
and strategies.

We develop the capability to deliver our strategies and
eliminate organizational barriers.

### Ownership

We accept personal accountability to meet our business needs,
improve our systems and help others improve their effectiveness.

We all act like owners, treating the Company's assets as our own
and behaving with the Company's long-term success in mind.

### Passion for Winning

We are determined to be the best at doing what matters most.

We have a healthy dissatisfaction with the status quo.

We have a compelling desire to improve
and to win in the marketplace.

### Trust

We respect our P&G colleagues, customers and consumers, and treat them as we want to be treated.

We have confidence in each other's capabilities and intentions.

We believe that people work best when
there is a foundation of trust.

## *Our Principles*

### We Show Respect for All Individuals

We believe that all individuals can and want to
contribute to their fullest potential.

We value differences.

We inspire and enable people to achieve high expectations,
standards and challenging goals.

We are honest with people about their performance.

## The Interests of the Company and the Individual Are Inseparable

We believe that doing what is right for the business with
integrity will lead to mutual success for both the Company
and the individual.

Our quest for mutual success ties us together.

We encourage stock ownership and ownership behavior.

## We Are Strategically Focused in Our Work

We operate against clearly articulated and aligned objectives
and strategies.

We only do work and only ask for work that adds value
to the business.

We simplify, standardize and streamline our current work
whenever possible.

## Innovation is the Cornerstone of Our Success

We place great value on big, new consumer innovations.

We challenge convention and reinvent the way we
do business to better win in the marketplace.

## We Value Mastery

We believe it is the responsibility of all individuals to continually
develop themselves and others.

We encourage and expect outstanding technical mastery and
executional excellence.

## We Seek to Be the Best

We strive to be the best in all areas of strategic importance
to the Company.

We benchmark our performance rigorously versus the very best
internally and externally.

We learn from both our successes and our failures.

### We Are Externally Focused

We develop superior understanding of consumers and their needs.

We create and deliver products, packaging, and concepts that
build winning brand equities.

We develop close, mutually productive relationships with our
customers and our suppliers.

We are good corporate citizens.

We incorporate sustainability into our products, packaging
and operations.

### Mutual Interdependency Is a Way of Life

We work together with confidence and trust across business
units, functions, categories and geographies.

We take pride in results from reapplying others' ideas.

We build superior relationships with all the parties who
contribute to fulfilling our Corporate Purpose, including
our customers and suppliers, universities and governments.

### P&G's Actions Reinforce Its PVPs

Another future P&G CEO—Bob McDonald—said this about their
PVPs. "The more international, the more we acquire, and the larger we
become, the more important the PVP is because it's that center post. It is
what guides us."[6] Two P&G incidents underscore how its PVPs directed
them. One involved information gathering from a competitor in 2001,
and the second dealt with its refusal to pay a foreign customs official to
expedite transporting raw materials into an African country.

### Dumpster Diving

One of P&G's largest competitors was, and continues to be, the
British-Dutch company—Unilever. In 2001, some Procter & Gamble

employees hired subcontractors to find anything they could about their rival. Unilever discarded some information without shredding it, and the subcontractors were more than willing to wallow through dumpsters to collect it. P&G's potential legal argument could have been, "if you're careless enough to leave proprietary information in an unprotected trash can, you shouldn't complain if someone takes it." When the P&G CEO at the time—John Pepper—learned about the incident, he didn't consult the legal department to strategize how to use the information while limiting their liability. He retold the story saying, "It was the easiest decision I ever had to make. There was no decision." Pepper embodied West Point's Cadet Prayer's admonition of choosing the harder right instead of the easier wrong. He said, "When we became aware that we might be in violation of our policy, we had one thought in mind: 'Do the right thing, and do it now!'"[7] His first action was to quarantine the data and then contact the CEO of Unilever—Nial Fitzgerald—explaining what happened. P&G returned the information to Unilever, fired the employees who devised the scheme, and ultimately settled with Unilever, paying them $10,000,000 and agreed to have a monitor oversee that the information was not used by P&G. DePaul University ethicist—Laura Hartman—commented on P&G's behavior saying, "Procter & Gamble could not have handled this any better … What more could we expect Procter to do. They fired the people and went beyond that and told Unilever what they had done."[8]

### Efficiency v. Ethics

In a second scenario, P&G was expanding its Pampers business in Africa and wanted to produce them locally. The last thing they needed to complete the process was $250,000 worth of top sheet material. That top sheet couldn't be manufactured in the country, so P&G had to import it. Unfortunately, a customs official in that country refused to allow it across the border without P&G's paying him a $5,000 fee. P&G could have argued that this was more of a "facilitating" or "grease" payment to a low-level guard instead of a bribe to a foreign official to enter into a new contract. This could have set up a good argument that the nominal fee of $5,000 didn't constitute a violation of the Foreign Corrupt Practices Act. Instead of taking this easy way out, P&G refused to pay what it considered extortion, all while its foreign plant remained dormant. Over the next four months, Procter escalated its complaints up the president of the country. That president ultimately sided with P&G and allowed the top sheet to be delivered to the plant. John Pepper cited a previous P&G CEO—Ed Harness—who told employees he'd rather P&G go out of business in a country than compromise P&G's values.

### Value Proposition for a Values-Based Leader

This chapter answers the question of why leaders should care about values. The darker side showed companies going out of business when senior management disregarded decency and carried out corruption. The positive side made a strong business case for doing the right thing and taking a values-based approach to conducting business.

The remainder of the book explores six lessons that leaders should consider in developing their values-based organizations:

1. What role do leaders play in advancing their companies' corporate culture?
2. How do leaders create a positive work environment prospective employees want to join and stay engaged with?
3. What reasons do employees give about why they violated company rules and laws, and what can leaders do to minimize these risks?
4. How should leaders encourage employees and others to report problems internally before they spin out of control?
5. What are the regulatory and business reasons leaders should encourage their organizations to develop a strong culture of ethics and compliance?
6. What cautionary tales should leaders be aware of regarding white-collar crimes, and how they should act to minimize violations?

# How Do Things Get Done Around Here?

Organizations, whether they are for-profit, nonprofit, or just an association of two or more individuals, all have one thing in common. Someone or some group started them. Those people all had personal values, but the follow-up questions would be: (1) Were these values "good" or "bad"? (2) Were they incorporated into the organization's corporate culture? (3) Did they survive the succession of future leaders?

This chapter analyzes corporate culture by asking and answering three questions:

- What is it?
- Why do we care?
- How can we promote it?

Corporate culture has four separate elements:

1. Shared values;
2. Tone of the organization;
3. Procedural justice; and
4. A willingness to bring bad news forward.

Culture can build a competitive advantage that encourages hiring and retention. It can also create a toxic cesspool which employees can't wait to leave. The culture should be consistent throughout the organization and transcend geographic borders. There shouldn't be different approaches depending on whether an employee operates in the field or their headquarters (HQ).

The Health and Human Services: Office of the Inspector General (HHS:OIG) and the Department of Justice (DoJ) recognize the importance of developing an ethical culture. These followed the U.S. Sentencing Commission's call for organizations to encourage an ethical corporate culture and a commitment to compliance with laws. In addition to the regulatory rationale, there is a strong business case to be made for a robust organizational culture.

Organizations should try to measure their corporate culture, preferably with stand-alone surveys, instead of just having a few questions in a yearly engagement study. Finally, stories can be an effective way of reinforcing the organization's commitment to its corporate culture.

The chapter concludes with a case study discussing:

- The history of Johnson & Johnson's Credo;
- How it was applied during the Tylenol poisoning crisis in 1982; and
- Whether it is perceived differently today.

## #1—Culture Eats Strategy for Breakfast— (Management Guru Peter Drucker)

Louis Gerstner, former CEO of IBM, said:

> Until I came to IBM, I probably would have told you that culture was just one among several important elements in any organization's makeup and success—along with vision, strategy, marketing, financials, and the like…. I came to see, in my time at IBM, that culture isn't just one aspect of the game—it is the game.[1]

This chapter addresses three questions about corporate culture:

1. "What?"
2. "So What?" and
3. "Now What?"

## What?

Warren Buffett said, "…culture, more than rule books, determines how an organization behaves."[2] Competitors can reverse engineer policies, procedures, and even products, but unlike a copier, scanner, or Star Trek replicator, culture is unique and can't be duplicated. Richard Farmer, the founder of the Cintas Corporation, called culture its number one competitive advantage, acting as the glue that holds a company together and is more valuable than money in the bank.

While a starter culture is a vital ingredient in baking sourdough bread, it is just as important that an ethical culture gets baked into how a business is run. This can be the secret sauce that differentiates one company from another. But just as a saucier chef might make the difference between receiving a Michelin star or not, left unattended, a sauce may get scorched, spoiled, or curdled, making the entire meal inedible. This is effectively what happened to Greg Smith, one of the former vice presidents of Goldman Sachs:

> It might sound surprising to a skeptical public, but culture was always a vital part of Goldman Sachs' success. It revolved around

teamwork, integrity, a spirit of humility, and always doing right by our clients. The culture was the secret sauce that made this place great and allowed us to earn our clients' trust for 143 years.... I am sad to say that I look around today and see virtually no trace of the culture that made me love working for this firm for many years. I no longer have the pride, or the belief.[3]

Without properly nurturing the culture, employees can become disillusioned. After business scandals become headline news, associates no longer brag about their jobs at backyard barbeques or consider themselves "the smartest person in the room." They would rather skip over that tenuous timeline in their resume instead of sinking with that reputational ship. One of the final ingredients to Goldman's hot mess was when Smith overheard some of the firm's sales force targeting unsophisticated clients and calling them "Muppets." That whole cultural stew left a bad taste in his mouth.

Penn State Management Professor—Linda Treviño—divides corporate culture into four different components:

1. Shared values;
2. "Tone" of the organization;
3. Fairness; and
4. Willingness to bring bad news forward.

### Shared Values

"Executive leaders and supervisors must regularly show they care about ethics and shared values (including demonstrating that values are an important part of 'bottom line' success), and they must show that they care through words *and* consistent actions."[4] Leaders can espouse polite platitudes, but the real question for members of a values-based organization is "does management walk the talk," or is it just lip service? Peter Drucker is credited with saying, "Tell me what you value and I might believe you, but show me your calendar and your bank statement, and I'll show you what you really value." Who are you meeting and where are you spending your money? Talk—check. Walk—check.

How can companies operationalize their values? Two examples of this are L'Oréal and Zappos. L'Oréal has four key ethical principles:

1. Integrity;
2. Respect;
3. Courage;
4. Transparency.

The former Chief Ethics Officer of L'Oréal—Emmanuel Lulin—was well traveled, visiting all of the L'Oréal plants and offices worldwide during his tenure. One common conversation with facilities managers was whether they respected their employees. After they pledged allegiance to their employees, Mr. Lulin would ask to inspect the restrooms at their facilities. If dirty, where was the dignity? With water on the floor, what was the employees' worth? It was one thing to talk about respect, but how was the manager demonstrating it?

Tony Hsieh (pronounced "Shay"), the founder of Zappos, helped develop the company's 10 core values:

1. Deliver WOW through service;
2. Embrace and drive change;
3. Create fun and a little weirdness;
4. Be adventurous, creative, and open-minded;
5. Pursue growth and learning;
6. Build open and honest relationships with communication;
7. Build a positive team and family spirit;
8. Do more with less;
9. Be passionate and determined;
10. Be humble.[5]

Zappos could develop metrics for the first nine values, but how would it measure the tenth—"Be Humble." On its face, this may seem difficult to discern, but Mr. Hsieh had a trick to determine humility and respect:

A lot of our job candidates are from out of town, and we'll pick them up from the airport in a Zappos shuttle, give them a tour, and then they'll spend the rest of the day interviewing, Hsieh says. At the end of the day of interviews, the recruiter will circle back to the shuttle driver and ask how he or she was treated. It doesn't matter how well the day of interviews went, if our shuttle driver wasn't treated well, then we won't hire that person.[6]

This didn't mean just because someone was polite, they'd be automatically hired, regardless of their qualifications. It did mean that even if someone was highly qualified, disrespecting others would disqualify them from a position at Zappos. Hsieh recognized that skill alone wouldn't make a good hire. Common decency had to be factored into the cost-benefit equation. Fortunately, this doesn't have to be an expensive proposition. Stephen Olson writes, "Care costs very little. Respect costs less. Both are priceless in terms of engendering employees' positive attitudes toward an organization."[7]

Businesses whose actions contradict their stated culture are breeding grounds for cynicism. Values must be more than colorful posters with snappy mnemonic devices framed on company walls. Slogans that are initially trumpeted, then ultimately trumped by pressure to maximize profits, send a signal to employees. The organization understood what its aspirational values were; it just chose not to follow them. If the company doesn't put actions behind these words, employees would prefer not to have their time wasted with superficial training and meaningless memos.

The message should be consistent, even with diverse constituents on different continents. Policies shouldn't contain an "*" stating that the rules don't apply in certain geographic areas because "that's not how it's done there." A large parent company with many decentralized subsidiaries, facilities, and offices in divergent parts of the world may allow some different legal techniques about how business is conducted. Even acknowledging this possibility, corporate culture should remain constant, guiding partners like Polaris—their "North Star."

While executive leadership may work hard to establish a culture of integrity at headquarters, sometimes policies and communications get lost in translation as one moves further from the central office. Attention to culture needs to be active and continuous, especially in large organizations with distant outposts.[8]

How is this attitude applied in international settings? Before 1977, some U.S. businesspeople sowed their corrupted seeds in an untended garden of deceit. There wasn't even a common name for the weeds that were choking off the beautiful blossoms of their values-based organization. To paraphrase Juliet's plea to Romeo, "A bribe by any other name would still stink." Whether it is *mordida* (the bite in Mexico), *baksheesh* (a tip or gratuity in Turkey), *bustarella* (the little envelope in Italy), or any other term, they all stand for one thing. If you want to play, you've got to pay! In 1977, the United States criminalized this once-tolerated tactic by enacting the Foreign Corrupt Practices Act (FCPA). Anyone doing business in the United States could be fined and imprisoned for paying off a foreign official to obtain or retain business. The DoJ and the Securities and Exchange Commission would now address this thorny issue by inspecting the gardens and pruning the weeds.

When in Rome, you might want to eat like a Roman, but you shouldn't cheat like a Roman. Values-based leaders (VBLs or principled principals) need to establish a moral compass pointing toward their company's "true North." If they don't, there really is a limited role for rules. Using a sports analogy, football—also known as futbol or soccer in America—is the most popular game on the planet, played with many varying styles. One thing every fan, player, and coach in the world, even Ted Lasso, understands is that a yellow card means they are being cautioned. A red card is given for a particularly egregious violation or a second yellow card on the same player during that 90-minute game—called a fixture. Whichever way this sports equivalent to a scarlet letter is earned, that person is ejected and must immediately leave the playing field—called the pitch. VBLs need their employees across the globe to understand what constitutes yellow or red card violations and not just hope for a lenient referee. Consistently buying into and following the correct corporate culture should help mitigate the risk of relativism.

Sometimes, company policies differ from country practices. Determining which one to follow can cause conflicts. L'Oréal addresses this issue in its Code of Ethics:

> There may be instances when the guidance in this Code is at variance with the local law or customs of a particular country. If that is the case where local law or customs impose higher standards than

those set out in the Code, local law and customs should always apply. If, by contrast, the Code provides for a higher standard, it should prevail, unless this results in illegal activity.[9]

Following whichever standard is higher may be more difficult in the short term but will ultimately convince associates that their company is serious about maintaining its culture.

## Tone of the Organization

VBLs' messaging is an important step in promoting the companies' standards. Organizations can establish this trickle-down ethics with communication cascading from the top tiers of leadership to the newest hires at the lowest levels.

Managers and employees take their cues from these corporate leaders. Thus, DOJ and SEC consider the commitment of corporate leaders to a "culture of compliance" and look to see if this high-level commitment is also reinforced and implemented by middle managers and employees at all levels of a business.[10]

Principled principals can establish a system of rewards and punishments to motivate employees and shape the culture of the company. Unfortunately, there may be a perceptual divide between the "tone at the top," the "mood at the middle," and the "buzz at the base." In the movie *The History of the World, Part 1*, Mel Brooks repeatedly reminded everyone that "It's good to be the king." While the view may be wonderful from those heights, does the rest of the company really believe rulers relate to their problems?

In 1989, Japanese consultant Sidney Yoshida coined the phrase "the iceberg of ignorance." This glacial mass was a metaphorical mess, representing the view about what percent of the organization understood the problems of the company. The research concluded that only 4 percent of top managers, 9 percent of team managers, 74 percent of team leaders, and 100 percent of the staff knew about the company's concerns.

Time, industry, and geography may be different from Yoshida's original findings, but even with changes in these calculations, there can be a titanic disconnect between the problems that senior management at the tip of the iceberg are aware of and the different layers of the organization underneath the surface, just waiting to sink the company. A 2019 Grant Thornton Report on the value of corporate culture underscored this division. "While 76 percent of executives believe they frequently communicate their value system, only 31 percent of employees agree."[11]

Part of the differing perceptions is understandable, depending on what office you occupy. Those working in suites starting with the letter "C" may be responsible for thousands of employees. They don't necessarily have the business bandwidth to be aware of every potential violation within the company. Certainly not at the same granular level as those closer to the issue. They rely on subordinates to address the questions and alert those on higher rungs of the corporate ladder regarding systemic problems or those which pose a material threat to the company.

What about the "buzz at the base"? In Yoshida's iceberg analogy, this is where problem awareness is the greatest and could impact the highest percentage of employees. It also makes sense that the person partners pattern themselves after is their direct manager or their boss's boss.

> Leaders at every level serve as role models, and employees have more daily contact with their supervisors than they do with executive leaders. Supervisors are responsible for rewards and punishments, and they carry the message of how things are really done in the organization.[12]

While the sovereign may reign supreme, the serfs and peasants take their cues from the feudal lords and knights, one or two levels above them. Even with their full-throated support of "Long Live the King," they know who has a direct impact on whether their work lives will be pleasant, tolerable, or miserable. While the King may still be alive, you can hear the muted but meaningful murmur of "Whatever you say boss." Huzzah!

### Fair Treatment of Employees

"Companies demonstrate their good ethics to employees primarily through fair treatment. If a company passes the 'fair treatment test,' employees are more likely to be open to ethics and legal compliance initiatives and to cooperate in making them successful."[13] VBLs can demonstrate this even-handedness by following procedural justice, which the Justice Collaboratory at Yale Law School states is made up of four components:

1. Voice;
2. Respect;
3. Neutrality;
4. Trustworthiness.

Voice addresses a person's ability to tell their side of the story. Respect looks at whether they were treated with dignity. Neutrality explores whether the decision making appears to be unbiased and transparent. Trustworthiness analyzes if the trusting party (Trustor) believes the party to be trusted (Trustee) will act in their (Trustor's) best interest. A positive response to these four elements creates a virtuous cycle, which creates more trust in the system. Even though employees may not agree with a decision, if they believe they've been treated fairly, they are more likely to accept it.

How is justice translated into action? It is great when the code of ethics tells employees not to cheat on their travel and entertainment expense reports, but we start to believe it when we see top performers being fired for mis-vouchering meals and mileage. Organizations love high-potential employees (HIPOs). These superstars not only meet expectations—they crush them! UCLA coaching great—John Wooden—knew that results weren't the only measure of success ("the what"). Wooden and other VBLs dig deeper to see the means used to get there ("the how"). Former CEO of General Electric (GE)—Jack Welch—echoed this philosophy in the 2000 Annual Report to the Board of GE, when he divided leaders into four distinct groups:

Type I: shares our values; makes the numbers—sky's the limit! Type II: doesn't share the values; doesn't make the numbers—gone. Type III: shares the values; misses the numbers—typically, another chance, or two … but Type IV is the toughest call of all: the manager who doesn't share the values, but delivers the numbers; .... But we have to remove these Type IVs because they have the power, by themselves, to destroy the open, informal, trust-based culture we need to win today and tomorrow.[14]

VBLs can't publicly scold and then privately wink at toxic HIPOs. Regardless of their exceptional performances, these are the people who should be fired first. Netflix takes this philosophy to heart when forming its "dream teams." They are very willing to terminate "brilliant jerks" because they go against the company's core values. In 2007, Warren Buffett jokingly told a group of University of Florida MBAs how to deal with employees with questions surrounding their integrity, intelligence, and energy. "If they didn't have the first, the other two would kill them, because if they don't have integrity, you want them dumb and lazy."[15] Organizations aspiring to have an ethical corporate culture integrated throughout the company should follow GE, Netflix, and Warren Buffett's lead regarding Type IV employees. In the words of management guru Peter Drucker, "Skills can be taught. Morals can't."

VBLs have to apply company policies evenly to superstars and everyone else. If they don't, the organization will create a two-tiered system of justice. One for "just us" and another for "just them." Tolerating Type IV HIPOs who ignore policies creates a culture in which rules are irrelevant. All that matters is hitting the numbers. In that universe, the only motivation employees have will be to perform well enough so they can ignore the rules. Even though there may appear to be plenty of manure spread around, a corporate culture can't grow on this "Animal Firm" in which some are "more equal than others." Honest employees will refuse to plow that field.

### Willingness to Bring Bad News Forward

Compliance and ethics programs that encourage open communication play an important role in developing an organization's culture:

> Research also shows that having a robust compliance program contributes significantly to shaping an ethical workplace culture by making the organization's norms, values and ethical expectations

clear to all employees. In the most effective ethics programs, peers talk openly with each other, their supervisors and their direct reports about ethical issues and pass along helpful information.[16]

Companies can conduct random audits and have complex internal controls, but the people in the best position to identify potential problems are those closest to the issues. The question becomes, how do VBLs create an environment in which those who know, get the information to someone who can do something about it—investigate and correct? Values-based leaders encourage open communication.

> [O]ne of the key pieces to think about is what sort of reaction do my managers have when they are challenged? Are people comfortable bringing up a new idea? Are people comfortable admitting that they made a mistake? All of those component pieces are things that are going to tell you as an ethics professional whether or not you've got the kind of culture inside your organization that will ultimately allow you to get at issues early and fix them before they become front page news.[17]

## So What?

Now that we have an idea about what makes up corporate culture, the follow-up question is: "Why should values-based leaders care?" The answer comes in two shapes and sizes: (1) the regulatory explanation and (2) the business case.

### The Regulatory Rationale

U.S. regulators have seen the value of values in fighting corruption by strongly encouraging companies to develop effective compliance and ethics programs:

> Culture has always been important to how organizations operate. So why is it getting so much attention lately? One reason is that regulators have come to the realization that without a culture of integrity, organizations are likely to view their ethics and

compliance programs as a set of check-the-box activities, or even worse, as a roadblock to achieving their business objectives.[18]

In the world of espionage, "CIA" is the abbreviation for the "Central Intelligence Agency." In health care, CIA stands for a "Corporate Integrity Agreement." This is a negotiated agreement between the Health and Human Services: Office of Inspector General (HHS:OIG) and a health care provider accused of overcharging the government. The HHS:OIG has both a significant compliance carrot and a really big stick! It posed the rhetorical question, "Would the health care provider like to be reimbursed by Medicare and Medicaid for patient care?" If the answer was yes, which effectively meant the provider could stay in business, that organization was required to follow those guidelines.

A comprehensive CIA typically lasts five years and includes requirements to:

- Hire a compliance officer or appoint a compliance committee;
- Develop written standards and policies;
- Implement a comprehensive employee training program;
- Retain an independent review organization to conduct annual reviews;
- Establish a confidential disclosure program;
- Restrict employment of ineligible persons;
- Report overpayments, reportable events, and ongoing investigations or legal proceedings;
- Provide an implementation report and annual reports to HHS: OIG on the status of the entity's compliance activities[19].

The first set of HHS:OIG standards came out in 1998 for hospitals, and subsequent ones included clinical laboratories, durable medical devices, and other health care-related areas. One common theme from these guidelines was the importance of culture.

Fundamentally, compliance efforts are designed to establish a culture within a hospital that promotes prevention, detection and resolution of instances of conduct that do not conform to Federal and State law, and Federal, State and private payor health care program requirements, as well as the hospital's ethical and business policies. In practice, the compliance program should effectively articulate and demonstrate the organization's commitment to the compliance process. The existence of benchmarks that demonstrate implementation and achievements are essential to any effective compliance program. Eventually, a compliance program should become part of the fabric of routine hospital operations.[20]

What a great idea for principled principals! Culture would no longer be a fig leaf to merely cover up gaping loopholes in meeting regulations. This culture of compliance is seamlessly woven into the tapestry of routine operations through repeated good actions and moral excellence.

Other regulators, including the SEC, EPA, Federal Energy Regulatory Commission (FERC), and the Federal Acquisition Regulations encouraged organizations to develop an effective ethics and compliance program. The DoJ jumped on the regulatory bandwagon with a series of memos and evaluations about the effectiveness of corporate compliance and ethics programs. The DoJ underscored the importance of companies encouraging ethical behavior.

> Beyond compliance structures, policies, and procedures, it is important for a company to create and foster a culture of ethics and compliance with the law at all levels of the company. The effectiveness of a compliance program requires a high-level commitment by company leadership to implement a culture of compliance from the middle and the top.[21]

How VBLs deal with these questions will determine whether DoJ staff attorneys prosecute individuals, organizations, neither, or both.

Just like the HHS:OIG, the DoJ has several significant "sticks" to encourage real compliance. Would the company like the department to forego criminal prosecution altogether—a declination? If this were a Monopoly board game, that company could "Advance to Go" and get back to the business of conducting business. It might not collect $200, but at least it would be able to use a "Get out of jail free" card. If not an outright declination, what about an agreement to not prosecute (NPA), or at least a deferral in prosecution, pending cooperation with any government investigations, and no additional violations for the next few years (DPA)? Where a company lands on this Monopoly board depends upon how it answers the following three questions posed by assistant U.S. attorneys (AUSAs):

1. Is the compliance program well designed?
2. Is it applied earnestly and implemented in good faith?
3. Does the program work in practice?[22]

Negotiating declinations, DPAs, and NPAs is like a chess match of strategic moves between the government and the accused's senior leaders, general counsel, and outside attorneys. In this gambit, companies might be willing to sacrifice a hierarchy of pawns, knights, bishops, rooks, and even their queen. It is all done to protect the king and prolong the game.

Both the HHS:OIG and the DoJ guidelines and evaluations were based on Chapter 8 of the 1991 Federal Sentencing Guidelines for Organizations (FSGO). These common-sense recommendations discuss the need for VBLs to both encourage an ethical corporate culture and a commitment to compliance with the law. VBLs who promote an effective ethics and compliance program will be subject to significantly smaller potential economic sanctions. Companies that ignore these initiatives face financial fine multipliers.

(For a more in-depth analysis of the DoJ's Principles of Federal Prosecution of Organizations and Chapter 8 of the U.S. Sentencing Guidelines for Organizations, please review Lesson 5—"What Happens if a Leader's Company Gets in Trouble?")

### The Business Argument

Decreased penalties help demonstrate "the value of values," but the case study goes further than criminal fine reductions. Directors and officers have a fiduciary duty to benefit company shareholders. When they don't, these same shareholders can bring a civil derivative action against them on behalf of the organization. On a more positive note, there are some potentially significant business rewards to be earned by maintaining a culture that employees are attracted to and thrive in. In 2019, Grant Thornton and Oxford Economics surveyed 500 U.S. business executives and 500 employees. Their report found that "organizations that make the right investments in culture are more likely to see stronger business performances."

There are many other business benefits to maintaining a positive corporate culture. The CEO of Ethisphere—Erica Salmon Byrne—stated:

> [W]e can actually now demonstrate that there is a correlation between companies with a good focus on longterm-ism and a strong vision for the organization and their financial performance, so it becomes less about, oh, that's a nice to have and really much more about that's a need to have.[23]

The Ethisphere survey shows good things happening when the supervisors frequently talk about ethics and ethics and compliance. Employees were:

- Twice as likely to be comfortable approaching their managers with concerns;
- 90 percent more likely to believe their managers are committed to nonretaliation;
- 54 percent more likely to believe their co-workers are acting ethically; and
- 24 percent more likely to believe they have personal responsibility to make sure the company does the right thing.[24]

When managers never discuss ethics and compliance, employees are:

- Two times less likely to believe senior leaders are always acting ethically;
- 89 percent less likely to believe their managers support the company's nonretaliation policy; and
- 82 percent less likely to believe the company will conduct a full investigation of concerns that are raised.[25]

Focusing on culture reinforces the company's brand and reputation for being a great place to work. Employees are more likely to be engaged and happy, lowering health care costs. This can lead to lower turnover and the costs associated with recruiting new employees. Engaged employees are more likely to follow company policies, mitigating the company's exposure and risk associated with civil and criminal litigation. Finally, organizational culture can be tied to customer satisfaction and ultimately sales.

Walker and Soule used a nautical analogy to describe why culture is important to businesses. "Culture is like the wind. It is invisible, yet its effect can be seen and felt. When it is blowing in your direction, it makes for smooth sailing. When it is blowing against you, everything is more difficult."[26]

## Now What?

After defining corporate culture and making the case why we should care about it, the final question for VBLs might be, "How is it developed, nurtured, improved and passed down to future generations?" The original owner's vision can be an excellent starting point. "Founders and influential leaders often set new cultures in motion and imprint values and assumptions that persist for decades."[27] While a founder's vision of company culture may be fundamental, how does a company build on this foundation? Without consistent reinforcement through observable actions, employees may believe "culture" is the management catchphrase *de jour*. New boss, new business buzzword. So why should I spend time and effort learning it?

Developing and maintaining a corporate culture can be challenging in normal times when employees, new and, old are interacting with each other in the office daily. It can be even tougher when employees are working remotely from home.

> From the moment you start a new job, you're indoctrinated in the culture of your employer.... You absorb a company's values from walls covered in fundraising posters, sales leaderboards or inspirational leadership quotations. At least that's how it used to be. Now that so many employees work from home—and are likely to continue doing so even after the pandemic ends—corporate culture is no longer something that can be absorbed so easily by new employees watching and listening to how things are done, and then passing on those values through their own actions.[28]

Principled principals need to be more intentional in promoting their culture in a world with a hybrid workforce.

The following section discusses the "Now What" question, focusing on measurements and stories.

### The Metrics of Ethics

Ethisphere's three-volume report entitled "Insights From Our Culture Quotient Data Set" provides excellent insight into the importance of corporate culture and includes many suggestions about how to measure it. "Metrics (or lack thereof) tell employees—especially newer employees—what the company really cares about."[29] Surveys can play a key role in determining how employees perceive their company's corporate culture. Unfortunately, this can create a battle with other departments like Human Resources about whether you only get a few questions in a semi-annual engagement survey or can develop and implement a specific culture survey. Engagement surveys can provide companies with very useful information, but they don't typically shine a light on the culture questions addressing whether employees observed misconduct and were willing to report it. The Ethisphere report stated, "Instead, we recommend running a standalone culture survey. Not only does this yield better results, it also communicates to employees that the company takes culture seriously enough to conduct a survey specifically about it."[30] These surveys and small focus groups can also create an opportunity to have a meaningful dialog between the moderator and the participants. Employees and middle managers may be more open about potential problems, especially with an independent facilitator.

Effective training and communications are key components to improving the ethical culture within an organization. Answering certain questions will help determine program effectiveness:

- Have associates been successfully educated about the resources available for them to "raise their hand" and report potential problems?
- Is the messaging understandable, concise, and relevant to their positions?

- Do they trust that their managers are committed to nonretaliation and will thoroughly investigate and act on their concerns?

One way of communicating the company's commitment to culture is through sanitized cases and stories "ripped from the company's headlines."

(For a more in-depth analysis of training, please review Lesson 5— "What Happens if the Leader's Company Gets in Trouble?")

### Stories Have the Power to Make Children Go to Sleep and Soldiers Go to War

Culture contains both formal and informal elements. Some of these deal with rituals, myths, and stories.[31]

> Every business needs a great story to engage customers and employees alike. A story imbues a brand with corporate values, a sense of history and consistency…. Stories bond your team, help define your corporate culture, and give clarity to the mission at hand.[32]

Culture becomes embedded in the company through chronicling these sagas.

## Case Study 1.1—Johnson & Johnson and the Tylenol Crisis

One example of a legendary event reinforcing a company's commitment to culture was Johnson & Johnson (J&J) and its Credo. This document underscores the importance of all company stakeholders, not just shareholders. According to the Credo, J&J should first meet its obligations to patients, health care providers, employees, and the communities in which they live and work and be a good corporate citizen. If all these groups are satisfied, then stockholders should realize a fair return.

What's interesting about this is that before J&J went public in 1943, the drafter of the Credo and former CEO—Robert Woods Johnson—and his family were the "stockholders." The enduring theory is that if the company values its other contributors, the current and future shareholders will be fine financially. Fast forward 30-plus years and a subsequent J&J CEO—Jim Burke—had senior-level gatherings focused on making sure this document remained relevant. "At one Credo Challenge meeting, he (Burke) even suggested that managers rip the document off their office walls if they refused to acknowledge its importance—that's how seriously he took the mission of putting its tenets into practice."[33]

Burke was a values-based leader who took the Credo to heart, and it guided him through one of J&J's most difficult crises—the 1982 cyanide-laced Tylenol incident that killed seven Chicagoans. Up until that point, national recalls were very rare. Cost containers could have argued for a less expensive localized recall within the Chicago region, but Burke had all Tylenol removed worldwide. What's more remarkable is that before the recall was announced, Burke met with the heads of the FBI (William Webster) and the FDA (Arthur Hayes), and they both discouraged him from recalling the product.

> To Burke's surprise, both Webster and Hayes felt adamantly that a national recall of the product would constitute an overreaction at that time.... Burke recalled, "but I was still very concerned that this was not the right solution (to not recall), either from the point of view of the public, or from the point of view of my company's business. I knew that I had the right to pull the product, but I hated to be in the position of making two regulatory agencies uncomfortable."[34]

This could have been the pitch-perfect case study for naming that tune called "Plausible Deniability." One can imagine a different CEO who wasn't influenced by something like a Credo singing a sob song, "We wanted to recall, but the FBI and FDA begged us not to. Our hands were tied." J&J also reimagined Tylenol's packaging, with three "tamper-evident" seals offering additional protection to consumers. This all occurred at lightning speed within six weeks after the incident, with the recall, product reimbursement, and repackaging efforts costing approximately $100,000,000.

Some were pessimistic about whether Tylenol would ever recover.

I don't think they can ever sell another product under that name," Madison Avenue advertising genius Jerry Della Femina told *The New York Times*. "There may be an advertising person who thinks he can solve this and if they find him, I want to hire him, because then I want him to turn our water cooler into a wine cooler.[35]

Thanks to Jim Burke's values-based leadership, information transparency, ethical candor, and swift actions, even decades later, Tylenol occupies prominent shelf space in many medicine cabinets.

J&J had built up a significant "trust bank," receiving goodwill deposits from previous leaders. When it came time to make a huge withdrawal from that account, their trust ledger was still positive. One year after the incident, Tylenol had regained 85 percent of its preincident business and was once again the leader in the pain relief industry. The saying "Good Ethics is Good Business" was proven right again.

While J&J is an excellent company, no business is perfect. J&J had a rash of recalls and lawsuits after 2005 dealing with product lines including Children's Tylenol, DePuy hip replacements, Acuvue contact lenses, Risperdal, baby powder, and opioids. There seemed to be a change in the "look and feel" of the corporate culture. An anonymous former quality employee complained, "The whole dynamic was very stressful … *It wasn't Do your job the right way*, it was *Do your job fast*. Make it look good, and get it done as fast as possible."[36] It is doubtful Robert Woods Johnson or Jim Burke would have approved of the changed Credo culture. Many J&J stakeholders recognize and appreciate the good works of the company and the value of its products, including developing one of the vaccines to fight COVID-19.

While J&J still follows its Credo that was developed in 1943, in 2023, the company split into two separate ones—"Johnson & Johnson" and "Kenvue." J&J will focus on medical technology and pharmaceuticals. The new Kenvue company deals with consumer health and includes brands like Benadryl, Zyrtec, Pepcid, Neutrogena, and even Tylenol. The new values statement for Kenvue, developed 80 years after the original Credo, has a similar sentiment, but a more modern feel.

We stand for what's right, even when it's hard. Our work impacts consumers and colleagues, communities and generations, in daily rituals and in the moments that matter most.

This incredible responsibility means every decision and action we take is guided by integrity and quality. Because when we put people first, performance will follow.[37]

Maintaining Jim Burke's Credo Challenge for J&J or affirming the Values proposition for Kenvue will be one way to ensure these principles endure. If they don't, they should "rip it from their walls."

## Conclusion

Ted Koppel's 1998 commencement address to Stanford University speaks to culture in general, but is also applicable to organizations:

We will not change what's wrong with our culture through legislation, or by choosing up sides on the basis of personal popularity or party affiliations. We will change it by small acts of courage and kindness; by recognizing, each of us, his or her own obligation to set a proper example. Aspire to decency. Practice civility toward one another. Admire and emulate ethical behavior wherever you find it.... There is no mystery here. You know what to do. Now go out and do it![38]

# LESSON 2

# Who Works Here and Who Stays?

Values-based leaders need to hire and promote employees in sync with their company culture. First, they must find the right employees, then they need to hire and retain them. In the end, it may be necessary to let them go, but VBLs can do this in a humane way that maintains the dignity of the former worker.

This chapter focuses on three decisions regarding employment:

1. Join us;
2. Stay with us;
3. Leave us.

The first section investigates the hiring process and the perks sometimes necessary to attract good candidates. During salary negotiations, new employees may make close to, or even more, than established associates, creating salary compression, inversion, and tension.

Retention can be critically important because of all the costs associated with hiring new staff and the loss of institutional wisdom from departing ones. During the pandemic, employers had to be nimble and allowed employees to work from home. This can make it more difficult to build a sense of community within the organization. It can also allow some employees to cheat their companies by working two or more jobs at the same time.

Employers worked hard to encourage workers to return to the office, but some employees resisted. In 2021, almost 48 million left their jobs and looked for work elsewhere. Out of this group, many were disillusioned by their new positions and wanted to return to their old companies.

The concept of employee engagement is then discussed and can be divided into three subgroups:

1. Engaged;
2. Disengaged;
3. Actively disengaged.

Engaged employees use their discretionary energy to benefit the company. Disengaged ones have "quietly quit" and are doing just enough to not get fired. Actively disengaged workers want their companies to fail and act accordingly. Gallup estimated the global business loss due to disengaged and actively disengaged workers to be $8.8 trillion in 2023.[1]

The final section of the chapter discusses how a company lets someone go. Most employees operate without a contract and can be fired "at-will." This means they can be terminated for good cause, bad cause, or no cause at all. There are several exceptions to this rule:

• Public policy;
• Implied contract;
• Covenant of good faith and fair dealing; and
• Violating an antidiscrimination statute.

Bad ways to terminate someone is to "fake" fire them as an April Fools prank or actually fire a large group over a Zoom call.

The final section of the chapter calls on principled principals to encourage employee self-reflection by asking themselves questions that indicate their level of engagement, performance, and resilience:

• Was I excited to work last week?
• Could I use my strengths at my job?
• Do I have a chance to do something I love?

# #2—"Should I Stay, or Should I Go?"— The Clash (1982)

*Would I ever leave this company? Look, I'm all about loyalty. In fact, I feel like part of what I'm being paid for here is my loyalty. But if there were somewhere else that valued loyalty more highly, I'm going wherever they value loyalty the most.*

—Dwight Schrute—The Office

## Introduction

Who has the most bargaining power in the employer–employee tug-of-war for work? That depends whether we're in a market with more jobs than prospective employees, or one in which if you don't take the job offer immediately, there's a line of people behind you eager to accept. The COVID-19 pandemic saw both scenarios within a short time span. In March of 2020 the world stopped. Government mandates closed businesses, restaurants, bars, hotels, movie theaters, sporting events, and life in general. No customers meant no money, and many companies took drastic measures to survive. This included across-the-board salary and benefit reductions along with forced furloughs and layoffs. Working from home (WFH) was the only way many employees could conduct business, and Zoom meetings replaced in-person contact with customers and colleagues. In the early days of the pandemic, we didn't know much about this deadly disease except what we learned from Boris Johnson, John Oliver, and viral TikToks about spending at least 20 seconds washing our hands, not touching our eyes, nose or mouth (the "T-zone" on your face), and "vampire coughing" into our elbows.

According to the June 2020 Bureau of Labor Statistics, due to massive layoffs, there were almost five (4.9) unemployed people for every job opening. Things looked bleak, but a series of government bailouts and stimulus checks allowed both businesses and individuals to stay afloat over the short term. Scientific research and technology raced at "Warp Speed," developing tests and vaccines to reduce the risk of serious illness and death. By 2022 the world looked very different than it did in 2020. Unfortunately, over one million Americans and over six million people worldwide have died because of Covid.

Even considering this tragedy, the job market changed dramatically over the two years since 2020. Instead of five people for each opening, there were now two jobs for every unemployed person. Signs pleading "Help Wanted" and "We're Hiring" were on display everywhere, and many interested in working seemed to have multiple options. Economic uncertainty may flip the script again, this time favoring employers. "Workers of a certain age and attitude will have to reckon with the coming recession. Rising inflation and a market downturn guarantee layoffs. The days of expecting employers to be grateful for your application will be gone soon."[2]

Values-based leaders need to understand this hiring-firing cycle, which is divided into three categories:

1. Join us;
2. Stay with us;
3. Leave us.

## Join Us

After a company determines it needs new blood, either to replace staff that left or to expand, it will draft the job description and start the hiring process. Both VBLs and prospective employees need to determine whether the job is a good fit regarding both skill set and culture.

### Perks

A job market that favors applicants may create an escalating arms race between companies competing for the same people. On top of the standard compensation package of salary, health care, and retirement benefits, there can be a treasure trove of perks to attract the best and the brightest to join their business. One can imagine a recruiter saying things like:

In addition to our on-site climbing wall, we've got foosball tables, free massages, lunches, and a cupcake food truck. Not enough? How about concierge level services that take care of the nasty chores you'd normally do on the weekends. Now you can watch your kids play soccer on Saturday without having one eye (or maybe both eyes) on your cell phone? Want more? You can bring your children to work and have them taught in education pods. Have a dog at home? Rover can come to the office too.

## Salaries

"While *Forbes* says job seekers should be upfront about asking how much the pay is, tension can cause some seekers to defer out of fear of losing the offer before it's even made."[3] Salaries used to be the dirty little secret no one was supposed to discuss. But now, with sites like Salary.com, Glassdoor, PayScale, Indeed, SalaryList, Salary Expert, and even the Bureau of Labor Statistics, the puzzle has been solved, and applicants now know exactly where they weigh in on the wage scale. If HR makes an offer considered too low, the applicant may not even bother countering. They'll just pick up their marbles and go play in a different sandbox. Values-based leaders interested in attracting and retaining the best talent may want to encourage offers closer to the top of the salary range.

> An employee who is offered what they are worth is not only more likely to accept the job offered, but is more likely to stay with the company longer out of loyalty. It also gives the company a larger pool of potential applicants to ensure they find the right person for the job.[4]

Higher starting salaries might create tension between newbie and veteran employees. It can demoralize established workers who are now making close to, or even less than, the shiny new things their boss just hired. Principled principals may want to address this type of salary compression or inversion by paying "job stayers" their market rate.

> Years ago, Netflix decided it shouldn't wait for good employees to be poached by competitors before offering them a raise—it should proactively pay its workers what they could make elsewhere. The best employees were rewarded for their loyalty, not penalized for sticking around.[5]

This type of meritocracy should reduce the financial incentive for employees to look elsewhere.

After the employee is onboard, we shift our attention to retention.

## Stay With Us: "Those Who Don't Know the Value of Loyalty Can Never Appreciate the Cost of Betrayal"—(Anonymous)

VBLs understand that employee turnover can be expensive, and replacing someone may cost between one and two times the salary of the person who left. The different outlays include:

- Money and time associated with advertising, interviewing, and screening prospective employees;
- Onboarding and training new staff;
- Lost:
  - Productivity;
  - Client relationships;
  - Institutional knowledge;
  - Sunk costs associated with training and developing employees who have left the company;
- The learning curve and errors new employees may make;
- Co-workers considering options after wondering whether the company is still a good place to work.

These are some of the financial reasons to retain qualified employees. How does loyalty factor into the equation?

### History of Work in the United States

Post-World War II, veterans from the Greatest Generation flooded the job market. There was an implied quid pro quo that if the wage earner worked hard, values-based leaders would reciprocate and take care of them. Worker's careers spanned an era of lifetime employment, good health care, a second car, vacations, and to the ability to educate their children. In addition to retiring with gold watches, they had pensions to make their golden years more comfortable. They defined themselves by their jobs and company loyalty was considered a virtue.

This relationship used to seem more personal. Almost familial. Now it's more transactional. Even considering expenses associated with hiring and retention, some companies may think—"You work until the end of the month, we pay you, and we're even! If you can get a better job somewhere else, have at it. If the company can find a better worker, maybe it should?" In Studs Terkel's 1974 book *Working*, one character—Larry Ross—represented this more cynical take on spending your entire career with the same company out of a sense of duty:

> The most stupid phrase anybody can use in business is loyalty.... Who is he loyal to? It isn't his country. It isn't his religion. It isn't his political party. He's working for some company that's paying him a salary for what he's doing. The corporation is out to make money. The ambitious guy will say, "I'm doing my job. I'm not embarrassed taking my money. I've got to progress and when I won't progress, I won't be here. The shnook is the loyal guy, because he can't get a job anyplace else."[6]

There seems to be a new definition of loyalty and it's not necessarily tied to longevity. This revised pledge of allegiance is measured by the employee's effort while on the job and speaking well about the company once they've left. Principled principals may promote a better postemployment relationship by developing alumni programs.

> Many companies, including Accenture and McKinsey, have found that staying close to a strong alumni community offers practical benefits in the form of existing client growth and referrals. But it's also a way for organizations to show their commitment to each employee as a person.[7]

### Remote Work

Once the government closed offices in response to the pandemic, those who could work from home had to figure out how to do it effectively.

Converting that hall closet into a tiny office was a first step. Learning how to mute both the audio and the webcam during Zoom, Teams, or WebEx meetings was next. Trading your business casual khaki slacks for sweatpants and pajama bottoms came after that. Employers were unsure how home-based work would impact productivity. They found out in April of 2021 that WFH could also stand for—"Worth From Home"—with remote employees reporting a 9 percent increase in efficiency compared to those operating out of the company's offices.[8] Regardless of the positive statistics, according:

> to a Future Forum survey, this skepticism toward work from home tends to come from older leaders in their 50s and 60s. Leaders under 50 are much more accepting of hybrid and remote work and focus on how to do it well.[9]

Employees were happy not paying rising gas prices or downtown parking rates. They also saved precious time. It was much quicker to roll out of bed and onto their couch instead of making a lengthy commute to their headquarters. Some employees were reluctant to return to the office because they were concerned about catching the coronavirus and passing it to their unvaccinated young children, an immuno-compromised friend, or a relative. After 18 months of the pandemic, 76 percent of employees wanted to work outside the office, some of the time.

The ability to work remotely opened new opportunities for employees—operating anywhere in the world that had decent Wi-Fi. This could be attractive because the cost of living is significantly cheaper in Peoria, Illinois, Tuscaloosa, Alabama, or Tijuana, Mexico, compared to New York, Chicago, the District of Columbia, or San Francisco. Previously, companies might have offered staff members a premium on top of their base pay to compensate for the higher living costs in expensive cities. Could companies save money by cutting salaries for these relocated remote workers? Perhaps, but employees may resent this reduction.

> Now, after more than a year of adjusting to remote work and remaining productive—in some cases increasing their hours— more people are questioning why their value is based on their

geographic coordinates.... While working from home, she's (a Facebook worker) doing the same amount of work but saving the company money because she no longer gets perks such as free, on-site dry cleaning and meals.... "Any loyalty I had for the company went out the window," Mr. Pedersen said. "My contract states a certain number and that's what I'm valued at whether I live in Mississippi or Mars."[10]

A company might also save money by moving into offices with a smaller footprint, but that would have to wait until its lease could be renegotiated.

### Building Relationships Remotely

While remote work may improve productivity, VBLs understand it's more difficult to develop a rapport with teammates over Zoom than in person. Poking your head into a colleague's cubicle with a quick question is much easier than scheduling a formal meeting on Microsoft Teams. "For those worried about their ability to connect, there is some good news: Research demonstrates that colleagues who work remotely can develop the same levels of trust as those working face-to-face—it just takes longer."[11] Instead of jumping right into the agenda at the beginning of an online meeting, values-based leaders might enter the online room a few minutes early to get to know colleagues and staff on a more personal level. This could give them context about why someone "can't take video calls at a certain time of day because of noise issues, or that you leave early on Thursdays to care for a family member."[12]

Instead of conducting an exit interview after someone has accepted a new job, principled principals should consider performing periodic "stay interviews." These discussions differ from traditional quarterly performance reviews. "'A stay interview is more focused on the intangibles, like morale and company culture,' says Garrett Garcia, vice president of the Tampa-based creative agency PPK which began conducting stay interviews before the pandemic."[13] These check-ins can expose potential reasons employees may want to leave an organization and give leaders a chance to change the (mis)perceptions.

Unfortunately, distance can also lead to distrust.

> If you are sitting at home and not really sure whether people you work with are doing their jobs, you start to think, "If we are not all working for the good of the team, I am just going to work for myself." "Instead of a cohesive group, you become five individuals," says Russell Haines, associate professor of information technology and decision sciences at Old Dominion University.[14]

One way to combat this is for VBLs to promote regular status updates. "If I see what people are doing, I have more trust that they are working, and it makes me want to work harder."[15]

### Out of Sight, Out of Mind Can Lead to Mischief

It was always possible for employees to be physically present at work but goof off like "The Office's" Creed Bratton (portrayed by Creed Bratton), playing spider solitaire on his computer all day long. The only skill they needed was to quickly minimize the card game and simultaneously pull up an Excel spreadsheet in case a nosey regional manager like Michael Scott stopped by to chat. These lazy loafers might even try to work an online side hustle during business hours. Fortunately, competent IT staff should be able to catch this misbehavior by monitoring network traffic.

Working remotely can make it easier for these duplicitous double dippers to go undetected. There's an online support group that gives guidance about how to deceive two employers at the same time.

> "It's two jobs for one," says a 29-year-old software engineer who has been working simultaneously for a media company and an events company since June. He estimates he was logging 3 to 10 hours of actual work a week back when he held down one job. "The rest of it is just attending meetings and pretending to look busy." He was emboldened by a new website called Overemployed. Started by two tech workers this spring, it aims to rally workers around the concept of stealthily holding multiple jobs.[16]

Cheating tips include declining meeting requests, citing a lack of bandwidth. If that isn't possible and two meetings are scheduled simultaneously, log onto one with your computer and another via phone. What happens if a worker gets called to give their thoughts at the same time during both meetings? No problem. Just leave one meeting, answer the remaining question, then rejoin the dropped call, apologizing for "Network problems."

### Return to Office

In 2021, senior officials were almost three times more interested in returning to the office than other employees.[17] It looked like workers were enthusiastically posting Instagram photos of themselves at concerts and sporting events or helping set box office records at "The Super Mario Brothers Movie" or "Barbie" premieres. They're willing to do everything they did prepandemic except go back to the office.

> What is holding up the return to the office right now? Plenty of workers simply don't feel like it. They're dining at restaurants, going to movies and taking trips, but offices aren't on their itinerary. That is delivering a reality check for bosses, who've been hoping the plunge in Covid-19 cases meant workers would finally—finally!—come back.[18]

Leaders felt a bit betrayed by this behavior, considering everything they did to retain workers at the beginning of the pandemic. "'The amount of effort and energy that was put into ensuring nobody lost their job—that we made the proper adjustments to weather the storm—people just don't remember those things,' he says. 'You have that lack of loyalty.'"[19] Disney CEO—Bob Iger—believed returning to the office was critical for creative cooperation. In a January 9, 2023 memo to Disney employees, he wrote:

> As you've heard me say many times, creativity is the heart and soul of who we are and what we do at Disney. And in a creative business like ours, nothing can replace the ability to connect, observe,

and create with peers that comes from being physically together, nor the opportunity to grow professionally by learning from leaders and mentors.[20]

In the 1942 movie *For Me and My Gal*, Judy Garland sang a popular World War I song, "How 'Ya Gonna Keep 'em Down on the Farm (After they've Seen Paree)?" The modern take on this might be—"How 'Ya Gonna Get 'em Back to the Office (After They've Worked From Home?)" Behavioral scientist Dr. Gleb Tsipursky confirmed this phenomenon:

> This situation illustrates the potent influence of the status quo bias. This bias, deeply entrenched in our human psyche, inclines us towards maintaining current states or resisting change. Employees, having tasted the fruits of flexible work, felt averse to relinquishing these newfound freedoms.[21]

Some associates who were given an ultimatum to return to work or leave the company—left. "You're not going to get me on the train for two hours for free bagels," says Jason Alvarez Schorr, a 36-year-old software engineer who quit his job in New York in January, when his former employer signaled an office return was imminent.[22] A survey by Unispace found that:

> nearly half (42 percent) of companies with return-to-office mandates witnessed a higher level of employee attrition than they had anticipated. And almost a third (29 percent) of companies enforcing office returns are struggling with recruitment. In other words, employers knew the mandates would cause some attrition, but they weren't ready for the serious problems that would result.[23]

In 2022, a Pew Center Research Poll found that 61 percent of telecommuters were doing so by choice, not for fear of Covid. "Among this group, more than three-quarters simply said they prefer working from home."[24]

### The Great Resignation

In 2021, a record number of workers (47.8 million) left their jobs.[25] Some resigned for better-paying jobs with competitors. Others started their own business or survived by doing gig work. "Many are getting by on a spouse's income by moving in with family, or simply making do with less."[26] Another group was just burned out and re-evaluated what work meant to them.

> One human resources manager called it the "Great Reflection" wherein people are "taking stock of what they want out of a job, what they want out of employment, and what they want out of their life." More often than not, workers are not content with labor that is unsatisfying, low-paying, and potentially harmful. And Gen Z has not been shy about detailing these expectations to employers and on social media.[27]

TikTok was filled with young employees celebrating leaving their jobs with "Quit Toks." Another group commented on the concept of "dream jobs" being more like nightmares. In 2019, voice actor—Casey Hamilton—played dual roles in an eight-second Internet video. The initial clip showed him posing as an earnest moderator, asking an off-screen person, "So tell us, what's your dream job?" Cut to his doppelganger wearing sunglasses and answering in a fake British accent, "Darling, I've told you several times before, I have no dream job. I do not dream of labor." This statement launched numerous lip-synched copies found on YouTube and TikTok. Both sets of posts are indicators of a general malaise and disdain for unsatisfying work.

### The Great Regret

Sometime between 43 BC and 17 AD, the poet Ovid wrote, "*Fertilior seges est alenis semper in agris*" (the harvest is always more fruitful in another man's fields). This sentiment was changed to "the grass is always greener on the other side of the fence" and is attributed to The Kansas Farmer, February 1917. Both sayings speak about coveting things you can see but don't possess. That stuff over there *must* be better than what you currently have. That's the attitude some employees developed regarding work when they decided to switch jobs.

What they found out is that their old grass may have been the "greenist" around. According to a 2022 survey by "the Muse," "almost three-quarters (72 percent) of them (job switchers) experienced either 'surprise or regret' that the new position or new company they quit their job for turned out to be 'very different' from what they were led to believe."[28] Almost half of that group suffered "shift shock" and tried to get their old job back.

Some values-based leaders understand it may only take new employees a few weeks to figure out they made a mistake. This can be costly to both the company and the worker. One way of dealing with this was to pay employees to quit shortly after they were hired. That was the strategy the CEO of Trainual—Chris Ronzio—employed:

> "It's important to know really quickly if we've found the right people," he (Ronzio) says.… "If someone knows a week or two in that this is not their long-term place or position, it gets more expensive to replace them as they take on more work and responsibility. By offering new hires $5,000, we give them the opportunity to opt out after two weeks if they have any sense of doubt." Ronzio borrowed the idea from Zappos, which gave employees what it called "The Offer": $1,000 to quit about a week into its immersive onboarding process.[29]

One option for dissatisfied employees is to return to their old company. This career carousel conjures up a song from the 1979 movie, "All That Jazz," when Peter Allen sings "Everything Old is New Again." These recycled workers are called "boomerang employees," and there are several advantages values-based leaders should consider about re-employing returners.

> Hiring managers tend to focus on asking high performers to return, because there's less risk of them leaving or not succeeding in the role compared with someone completely new to the organization, says Abbie Shipp, a management professor at Texas Christian University who specializes in employee engagement

over time. And in today's labor crunch, hiring managers want nothing more than a safe bet.[30]

Depending on how long the "boomeranger" worked at another company, they may bring a different perspective upon their return. This new skill set and insight can be a valuable asset to the old company.

## Case Study 2.1—A Retailer Retells the Tale About the Link Between Ethics and Engagement

The following blog post was from a large retailer's former Chief Ethics and Compliance Officer (CECO). It has been anonymized and reprinted with the company's permission.

> Every year, [company] employees worldwide are asked to participate in surveys that measure their "engagement" levels as employees of the company. This survey data, in turn, is used for "action planning" activities that seek to improve the employee experience and eliminate barriers to employee engagement.
>
> More than simply measuring how "happy" our employees are, we focus on engagement because it has been statistically proven that our profitability and performance as a company are directly tied to employee engagement levels. The more engaged our employees are, the more likely they are to innovate, take pride in their work and make the extra effort necessary to deliver a terrific customer experience. But what about employee ethics? Is there a connection between an employee's engagement level and their likelihood to behave in an ethical manner? A recent letter from a former employee offers a compelling case study.
>
> Earlier this month, the leaders of our Loss Prevention (e.g., theft) team received a heartfelt letter from a person who had worked for [the company] nearly a decade ago. He described in great detail how much he loved working for [the organization] and how he had become known among customers and co-workers for being the very best at what he did. His story had all the earmarks of a highly engaged employee—exactly the type of experience we would like every one of our…people to have.

As the letter went on, the employee described how he also became known for something that wasn't part of his job description per se. The employee found he could spot a shoplifter from across the store simply by observing their nervous ticks and bizarre shopping habits. He would keep an eye on these people and alert his co-workers so that the shoplifters could be legally and safely stopped in the act. By his count, he had personally prevented more than $4,000 in merchandise from walking out of the store in the coats and purses of would-be shoplifters.

Unfortunately, this extra effort apparently went unnoticed by his store leadership team. The employee put a tremendous amount of "discretionary energy" into cutting the store's theft losses and with great success, but that success was neither recognized nor rewarded as the employee had hoped. And so, the employee stopped caring. He no longer bothered with shoplifters, no matter how obvious. He even looked the other way when fellow employees pocketed merchandise.

Over time, the employee lost his passion for [the company] and left ... to pursue a different career. That was ten years ago. Last week we received his letter along with a check for $700, an amount he thought was greater than the value of the merchandise he had knowingly allowed to be shoplifted after his engagement level had dropped. His failure to prevent those thefts haunted him for a decade and ultimately prompted him to *pay* [the company] for the lost product.

We returned the check to our former employee, of course, and thanked him profusely for this stunning example of personal integrity. I only regret that he isn't still a member of [our] team. Who knows what value he could have added to our company if given the encouragement he was looking for?

The CECO recognized the missed opportunity to retain a valuable employee. Sometimes, even a small gesture will be enough to recognize an associate and thank them for going above and beyond their job responsibilities. This can result in an engaged, ethical team member who is loyal to the organization and willing to use their discretionary energy to support it.

## Case Study 2.2—Employee Engagement Demonstrated by "Office Space"

The terms loyalty and engagement are not interchangeable. Janice Bellace, a Professor of Legal Studies and Ethics at Wharton, holds:

> "Loyalty implies something more about the relationship" being reciprocal, she said. "If you're at a company and feel productive and properly treated, you may still go to another company if they pay you 20 percent more. But if people feel very engaged and well treated, they not only will feel productive, they will want to stay.[31]

While loyalty may measure a person's willingness to come into work that day, engaged "employees are mentally in the zone, ready for action."[32] The three categories of engagement—engaged, disengaged (or not engaged), and actively disengaged can be demonstrated by characters from the 1999 movie *Office Space*.

### Engagement

Gallup's 2023 annual survey found 32 percent of the U.S. employees surveyed were engaged, down from 36 percent in 2020.[33] Principled principals understand these employees are typically healthier, safer, and more productive than others.

> Engaged workers stand apart from their not engaged and actively disengaged counterparts because of the discretionary effort they consistently bring to their roles. These employees willingly go the extra mile, work with passion, and feel a profound connection to their company.[34]

The Office Space character that demonstrates engagement is Brian (played by Todd Duffey), the highly caffeinated, speed-talking waiter trying to upsell everyone "Pizza Shooters, Shrimp Poppers or Extreme Fajitas." While his restaurant—Chotchkie's—only required its waitstaff to wear 15 pieces of flair, Brian more than doubled that by filling the front and back of his suspenders with 37 items of buttons, bling, and blinking lights. The only person with more flair than Brian might be a former professional wrestler—Ric "The Nature Boy" Flair.

### Disengaged

Disengaged employees will do their job, follow the rules precisely, and reluctantly come to work the next day. They may stay at a job not out of a sense of passion but a combination of inertia and fear. In 2022, Gallup estimates this group to be approximately 51 percent of the U.S. workforce.

> Jim Harter, chief scientist for Gallup's workplace and well-being research, said workers' descriptions of "quiet quitting" align with a large group of survey respondents that he classifies as "not engaged"—those who will show up to work and do the minimum required but not much else.[35]

Gen Z doesn't have a monopoly on the concept. Different generations had their own names for this. It could be called "slacking off" or "coasting" for Gen Xers or "having boundaries" for Millennials. Some indicators of disengagement and quiet quitting include withdrawal, poor communication, silence, apathy, absenteeism, missing deadlines, and cynicism. Values-based leaders should try hard to convert these disengaged workers into engaged ones.

The Office Space character representing a disengaged employee is Joanna (Jennifer Aniston). When the Chotchkie manager Stan (played by Office Space writer and director Mike Judge) brings up Joanna's lack of flair by only wearing 15 pieces, he chastises her by saying,

> Look, we want you to express yourself, okay? Now if you feel that the bare minimum is enough, then okay. But some people choose to wear more and we encourage that, okay? You do want to express yourself, don't you?[36]

After she is repeatedly badgered by Stan about her commitment, tempers flare, and she doesn't quit quietly. Joanna digitally expresses herself and loudly leaves her soul-crushing job with some real flair.

### Actively Disengaged

Actively disengaged employees are miserable and hate their jobs. George Carlin's joke about this was, "Oh, you hate your job? Why didn't you say so? There's a support group for that. It's called EVERYBODY, and they meet at the bar."[37] They dread going to bed at the end of the weekend because they'll have to go to work the next day. This is known as the "Sunday Scaries."

It is one thing to internalize this feeling, but actively disengaged employees want to do more. They try to "poison the well" and damage the company that is hurting them. Gallup's 2022 survey estimated that 17 percent of employees fell into this category. Principled principals shouldn't tolerate this type of behavior and should strongly consider terminating them.

The Office Space's Peter Gibbons (played by Ron Livingston) is actively disengaged from his job at the fictional company—Initech. He confesses:

> So I was sitting in my cubicle today, and I realized, ever since I started working, every single day of my life has been worse than the day before it. So that means that every single day that you see me, that's on the worst day of my life.[38]

Peter's perpetual "case of the Monday's" fed his general job funk. This combined with hatred for his boss—Bill Lumbergh (played by Gary Cole)—put in motion a plan to plant a virus on the company's computer and defraud it out of a small fraction of a penny per transaction (similar to the tactic Richard Pryor used in the movie *Superman III*). Originally thinking the scheme would only generate unnoticeable sums per day, Gibbons and his band of brothers (Michael Bolton and Samir Nagheenanajar) were shocked when the first day's haul was $305,326.13. A combination of remorse and fear of jail time led Peter to slip a confession and $300k worth of travelers checks under Lumbergh's door. In a plot twist, perpetually displaced Swingline stapler lover Milton (played by Steven Root) walks into Lumbergh's unlocked empty office, pockets the unnoticed checks, and burns the building down, including Peter's admission. At the end of the movie, Peter is seen enjoying his new job in construction with all the evidence of the fraud destroyed by the fire. Milton is caught lounging in an undisclosed tropical paradise, sipping a Pina Colada, even though he specifically ordered a Mai Tai. A disinterested waiter ignores Milton's mumblings, just like he was treated at Initec.

Actively disengaged workers not only jeopardize immediate sales but also can leave such a bad taste in the customer's mouth that many will never do business with the company again. In 2019, Gallup estimated that "actively disengaged employees cost the U.S. economy $483 billion to $605 billion each year in lost productivity."[39] The global impact is even more stark. Gallup estimates the cost of disengagement and active disengagement caused $8.8 trillion in lost productivity throughout the world in 2023.[40]

Actively disengaged employees are a logical group for VBLs to cull from the company. What is the best way to accomplish this?

# Just Leave

Unless you are a tenured professor, sports star, union member, or senior executive, you probably don't have a work contract that provides any protection against firing. Employees sign lots of papers during the onboarding process. While the paper pushing during orientation may look like a binding agreement, those pages typically don't guarantee their job for any set time. If anything, state law permitting, it may include a covenant not to compete. This means that if the employee leaves the company for whatever reason, they can't work for a direct competitor in the same field and geographic area for a set number of years. It will be interesting to see if the Federal Trade Commission outlaws noncompete clauses in the future.

### At-Will Employment

These noncontract employees are considered "at-will," meaning they can be fired for good cause, bad cause, or no cause at all. In the United States, all states except Montana recognize some form of at-will employment. Termination doesn't have to take a great deal of time or negotiation, as demonstrated by an August 2013 conference call by the CEO of AOL—Tim

Armstrong. He became upset with Abel Lenz, a senior executive at AOL. During the course of a few seconds on a group call, Armstrong admonished Lenz, telling him, "Abel, put that camera down now." A moment later, Armstrong followed up with "Abel, you're fired. Out."[41]

There are several exceptions to at-will employment:

- Public policy—these exceptions should be specifically expressed in a state's constitution or laws;
- Implied contract—include statements made by a supervisor like "you've got a job for life," or written assurances of continued employment in policies or employee handbooks;
- Implied covenant of good faith and fair dealing—requires just cause to terminate an employee;
- Violating an antidiscrimination statute—an employer cannot discriminate because of a person's race, color, religion, sex, national origin, age, sexual orientation, disability, or veteran status.

The legal rationale behind at-will employment focuses on the "doctrine of mutuality." While an employer can fire someone without justification, an employee can also quit for any reason. One of the more dramatic examples of resigning with flair involved Jet Blue flight attendant Steven Slater. On his last flight as an attendant, Slater reprimanded a passenger who attempted to retrieve her baggage in the overhead bin while the plane was still taxiing toward the gate. The unsecured bag struck Slater's head. He snapped, cursed out the passengers over the plane's intercom, grabbed a beer, and deployed the emergency slide. He used that as his means of escaping the plane and his 20 years of flying the not-so-friendly skies. Slater was later arrested and ultimately sentenced to one year of probation for criminal mischief.

Another example didn't have the same amusement park feel but portrayed Marina Shifrin's farewell to arms while interpretive dancing to Kanye West's song "Gone." She racked up almost 20,000,000 views on YouTube by September 28, 2013. Shifrin filmed herself at 4:30 a.m., working at a Taiwanese animation company. Her rave-worthy moves included a note to her boss on the video saying—"I quit." She turned out the lights, exited the office, and with one final note told the world "I'm Gone." Faced with the news of Shifrin's departure, her former company—Next Media Animation—filmed a mocking rebuttal video using the same Kanye West song. Her ex-boss and the remaining animators danced, laughed, and generally acted goofy, followed by the solicitation—"We're hiring." Even though this video only had one-fourth of the views of Shifrin's post (4,666,369 as of October 1, 2013), the dueling dances demonstrated the doctrine of mutuality.

If an employee is too frightened to quit in person, they can use the website "Cameo" to hire a TikTok influencer or former American Idol loser—William Hung—to soften the blow of leaving the team. Hung told one team:

> Christopher is going to put in the notice to leave the current job for a new job in two weeks. He found a new job. He'll miss all of you but you are all amazing so don't give up creating the life you want.[42]

Those interested in a harsher departure can hire Brian Cox (who played Logan Roy in *Succession*) for $689 for a 30- to 180-second message on Cameo. Mr. Cox's memorable missives tend to feature some choice expletives.[43]

So, when did U.S. executives change from paternalistic values-based leaders offering lifetime employment into cutthroat CEOs, figuratively chopping employee heads to improve the company's bottom line? The 1987 movie *Wall Street* might provide an answer. In the film, Gordon Gekko (played by Michael Douglas, who won an Oscar for Best Actor for this role) is a corporate raider looking for companies that are underperforming and have an undervalued stock price. Gekko is able to: (1) swoop in, (2) buy the company at a discounted price, (3) fire employees, (4) sell off divisions, and then (5) exit with a healthy profit. He repeated this legal legerdemain with the help of his Faustian apprentice—Budd Foxx (played by Charlie Sheen). Gekko's Mephistopheles is only stopped when Foxx refuses to let him "liberate" his father's company—Bluestar Airlines.

Management witnessed the success outsiders had in raising the stock price by downsizing and adopted this tactic themselves. The 2010 movie—*The Company Men*—demonstrated how this could be applied to the fictional company—GTX. That enterprise was founded by James Salinger (played by Craig T. Nelson), who needed to quickly raise its stock price to make it less attractive to a hostile takeover. Instead of selling the company-owned original Degas artworks, Salinger's solution was simply firing more people. One casualty was a senior executive—Phil Woodward—(Chris Cooper). Woodward worked his way from rags to riches, then back to rags again in the emotional roller coaster that was his business life. Throwing rocks at the corporate headquarters (soon to be replaced by a newer, larger, more expensive one), he bemoaned how his life was ruined while the earth kept turning. His character screamed— "You know the worst part. The world didn't stop. Newspapers still came every morning. The automatic sprinkler shut off at 6:00. Jeff, next door, still washed his car every Sunday. My life ended, but nobody noticed."[44] Phil Woodward died by suicide after this, demonstrating the life-and-death consequences downsizing can have on ex-employees.

### *Different Ways to Fire Employees*

On April 1, 2022, Reddit user—Savathun—explained, "My boss told me I was fired as soon as I got into work, laughed and walked off."[45] She spent several hours packing up her office and went home. There, Savathun received a call from that supervisor, asking where she was. She replied, "You fired me, why the h*** would I be at work?" Her boss claimed it was an April Fools prank and she should return to work immediately. Instead, she stayed home, complained to HR, and her supervisor was ultimately let go from the company. Savathun returned to work and received a $5.15 per hour raise, along with four bonus weeks of vacation. Now who is the April Fool?

In December of 2021, Vishal Garg—CEO of Better.com— demonstrated another bad way of communicating bad news. During a Zoom call with 900 employees (9 percent of the company's workforce), he explained, "'If you're on this call, you are part of the unlucky group that is being laid off,' Garg said on the call ... 'Your employment here is terminated effective immediately.'"[46] This language was lifted almost verbatim in one of the final episodes of "Succession," in which cousin

Greg fires American Television Network employees during an online call. This might be acceptable if employees are working remotely. It would be even more unfair to bring someone into the office for the first time just to let them go.

> Yet mass "Zoom firings" make headlines; to devastated workers, the news can feel like a compassionless blindside. There's no one-to-one chat in a side-office, no way to ask questions or process what's happened in the way there is with an individual, in-person conversation.[47]

Without a better justification, laying off people this way is just too impersonal.

The 2009 movie *Up in the Air* predicted this type of high tech termination. Ryan Bingham (George Clooney) was the job killing equivalent of the Grim Reaper. Bingham did the outsourced dirty work for bosses too afraid to fire employees themselves, but he did it personally, and the ex-employee left with some dignity. Bingham was assigned to show recent college graduate Natalie Keener (played by Anna Kendrick) how the job was done. Even in this pre-Zoom environment, she thought there was a better way. Why waste so much money on consultant airfares, hotels, meals, and booze when you could let people go via videoconferencing? After one of her victims took her own life, Keener learned, like Better. com's Garg, that communicating bad news during a troubling time required more of a personal touch.

Terminating an actively disengaged worker is easier to justify, but what happens when you have a good employee who needs to be let go for reasons not associated with performance (e.g., a financial downturn in the business)? While David Letterman's Late Show had a nightly Top 10 List, JetBlue's Chairman—Joel Peterson—demonstrated values-based leadership with his Top 10 "Do's and Don'ts" about how to fire with compassion:

- "Don't wait for a 'firing offense;'
- Do be willing to fire friends or family;
- Don't surprise people;

- Do prepare and practice;
- Don't hand off the dirty work;
- Do deliver the message immediately and clearly;
- Don't overexplain the decision;
- Do be human;
- Don't shift the blame;
- Do be generous."[48]

Some of the best advice is to be truthful. VBLs explain that it wasn't anything they did or didn't do. It was an unfortunate business necessity. After the initial shock, principled principals should provide strong references and use their network and contacts to help employees land their next jobs. Values-based leaders might even offer to speak with the employee's family, letting them know the circumstances surrounding the situation.

## Conclusion

So, how should VBLs deal with their staff? "Caring for employees as individuals is a powerful way to get them to care about your company. That loyalty sets your business up to be the strongest, fittest company equipped for survival."[49] Sometimes, a simple "thank you" by a leader can improve an employee's sense of their own worth and motivate them to do better. Gratitude can be even more effective when coupled with something tangible in the form of additional money, perks, or recognition.

The ADP Research Institution (ADPRI) conducted a 2022 survey of over 50,000 people worldwide. The biggest indicators regarding performance, engagement, resilience, retention, and inclusion weren't pay, location, mission, or even co-worker collegiality. The three most significant questions were:

1. "Was I excited to work every day last week?
2. Did I have a chance to use my strengths every day?
3. At work do I get a chance to do what I'm good at and something I love?"[50]

This research found employees who find fulfillment and excitement in their work are more likely to be productive and stay with the company longer than others. While it is unlikely that employees will find joy at work all the time, research by the Mayo Clinic suggests that workers who love what they do at least 20 percent of the time are less likely to be burned out.[51] Interestingly, there doesn't seem to be much marginal resilience after exceeding this 20 percent threshold.

So, what can values-based leaders do to improve this sense of joy and love of work?

> The boss's job isn't to create a fun place to work, he maintains. It's to provide employees with a greater sense of purpose. Work that's worth the effort—and worthy of loyalty—is about "being part of a team where you provide meaningful service that enriches the lives of others," Reichheld explains. The pandemic didn't create the problem of work that lacks meaning, he adds, but it did expose the problem.[52]

Employees who are recognized and rewarded for their loyalty can create a positive impact on their companies. Those who aren't may find better opportunities elsewhere.

# LESSON 3

# Why Do Good People Do Bad Things?

Values-based leaders need to understand why their employees are breaking rules and laws and how to minimize these risks. After discussing the Fraud Triangle, these motivations are broken down into eight separate categories, followed by possible solutions.

*Strict constructionists* technically comply with the laws but try to stay as close to the line as possible. Unfortunately, this doesn't leave any legal room if something unexpected happens.

*Incrementalists* are people who start down the slippery slope, one small step at a time. This is also referred to as "salami slicing" because the cut can be so slim that no one seems to notice it. Avoid taking that first step because it is very difficult to stop once started.

*Altruists* tend to cheat, not to benefit themselves but to help others. They steal for the organization, not from it. Even though their company appears to be the beneficiary, values-based leaders shouldn't accept the tainted gift from the employee. VBLs must reinforce the importance of ethics and compliance and not wink at violations.

*Prisoners of circumstances* have someone else's problems dropped in their lap. They didn't cause the concern, but it happened under their watch. They would like to wish the problem away, but principled principals should encourage employees to deal with them head-on, not try to sweep them under the carpet.

*Rationalizers* cheat up to the level that they can still consider themselves to be a good person. They believe:

- It is such a big company, no one will miss the amount I have taken;
- It is such a brilliant scheme, no one will ever find out;
- Everyone else is doing it.

Warren Buffett has said, the five most dangerous words in business might be "everyone else is doing it."

*Conformists* follow the group or an authority figure. Several social psychologists have conducted research demonstrating this:

- The Asch experiment;
- Milgram's study of obedience.

Values-based leaders need to encourage a diversity of thought and a willingness to accept challenges about how things are done at the organization.

*Browbeaten* employees are pressured by their bosses to achieve their goals that can't be realistically accomplished by acting ethically with the resources they have been provided. VBLs should establish S.M.A.R.T. goals:

- Specific;
- Measurable;
- Achievable;
- Relevant;
- Time-based.

*Hedonists* act out of a sense of pride, greed, and hubris. The rules apply to everyone else, or as Leona Helmsley said, "Only the little people pay taxes." Values-based leaders need to continuously promote sound ethical behavior in their employees and discipline those who break the rules.

# #3—Fraud Factor Motivations and Mitigations: Metaphors From Movies to Milgram

## Case Study 3.1—The Fraud Triangle

A trusted employee, who hasn't taken a vacation in years, wakes up in a hospital bed to the sounds of beeping monitors. The last thing the patient remembers was driving home from work and seeing a deer jump out of the bushes. After this—a loud thump, then everything went dark. Still in a foggy haze, many unanswered questions remained:

- **Who** found me?
- **What** am I doing here?
- **Where** am I?
- **When** can I get back to work?
- **Why** did this happen to me?

Another co-worker temporarily assumes the hospitalized employee's duties. The stand-in is first confused, then concerned about how the injured co-worker has been recording certain transactions. The numbers just aren't adding up. Digging deeper, the reluctant replacement unravels an embezzlement scheme that has been covered up for years. The company is the latest victim of "the Fraud Triangle," a phrase attributed to criminologist Donald Cressey. Other researchers have stretched, pulled, and reshaped this polygon into a Fraud Diamond and even a Fraud Pentagon, but the basic elements remain the same—motivation, opportunity, and rationalization.

Motivation means a fraudster believes they need more money. They're typically under a lot of financial pressure. Perhaps a spouse lost a job, or a relative is ill. Maybe they have an addiction to gambling, alcohol or drugs, or just like living beyond their means. They have a problem but can't share it with anyone else. So, what's the solution? This is when opportunity knocks, sometimes in the form of inadequate internal controls. The swindler understands the weaknesses of their company's checks and balances. They may have even designed them. An example would be allowing the same person to send out invoices and then open the payment envelopes. The customer paid what they believed was a legitimate bill, but the money was diverted to the employee's personal account—never actually hitting the company's books. This is a recipe for disaster because no one was looking over their shoulder. Check—no! Balance—no! Whenever possible, values-based leaders need to segregate duties within the office. They should consider rotating responsibilities and conducting random spot audits. And just because an employee refuses to take any time off doesn't mean they're loyal and dedicated. They might not want anyone else reviewing their activity, in order to prolong the fraud. Countless schemes have been revealed after employees were forced to take a vacation or ended up in the hospital because of an accident.

Rationalization occurs when people rattle off a list of reasons, at least to themselves, why they're acting a certain way. They may feel underappreciated, trapped, or even a "team player." Whatever shape and size of the fraud, it can be very expensive to companies.

According to ACFE (Association of Certified Fraud Examiners) estimates, fraud costs organizations fully 5 percent of annual top-line revenue. This enormous cost is serious enough, but it is compounded by the fact that fraud is a hidden crime that erodes an organization's capacity from within. Consequences can go beyond monetary losses to inflict damage on morale, trust and transparency. These kinds of costs endure far beyond the triggering event.[1]

## Responding to Fraud

What is typically asked when potential problems are discovered?

Another variation of the five "Ws" come to mind:

1. "**Who** did this?"
2. "**What** were you thinking?
3. "**Where** will this problem lead us?"
4. "**When** will it stop?"
5. "**Why** didn't I find out about this sooner?"

These questions are understandable, but they're the wrong ones being asked at the wrong time. Principled principals pursue a better line of inquiry:

- "**Who's** in trouble?"
- "**What** can I do to help?"
- "**Where** do you need me?"
- "**When** will employees believe they can succeed, while staying within acceptable rules?"
- "**Why** didn't they trust me?"

To address this final set of questions, VBLs need to better understand why people act improperly, and what they can do about it. Many violators fall into one or more of the categories discussed earlier.

Strict constructionists;
Incrementalists;
Altruists;
Prisoners;
Browbeaten;
Conformists;
Rationalizers; and
Hedonists.

This chapter analyzes each of these fraud considerations and presents how values-based leaders can respond to limit them.

### Strict Constructionists—"Those Who Favor a Narrow Conservative Construction of a Given Document or Instrument."

On May 9, 2022, Elon Musk tweeted, "Like I said, my preference is to hew close to the laws of countries in which Twitter operates. If the citizens want something banned, then pass a law to do so, otherwise it should be allowed."[2] Strict constructionists like Musk view laws as minimal lines in the sand. Just above it, you're in compliance. Below, it's a violation.

Picture a corporate contest to see which supervisor can spend the least amount of money on rule-following but still be in technical observance with laws, regulations, and policies. This race to the bottom might tick the legality box, but it doesn't leave any room for error. Using laser-like precision to just squeak over the protected precipice ("nano-compliance"?) doesn't answer the question—"How to calculate this risk when something unplanned occurs?" The formula seems to be:

> A "Spartan" approach to rule following + an unforeseen event = laws being broken.

Imagine trying to explain this logic, and the rules of the contest, to the Department of Justice as to why the company shouldn't be fined or indicted. It wouldn't go well.

So, is strictly following the laws enough? Let us go back in the Time Machine over 100 years ago and see an example of something that was "lawful," but "awful."

## Case Study 3.2—Why Didn't the Titanic Have More Lifeboats?

In 1912, the Titanic was designed to be "practically unsinkable." Its hull had 16 separate compartments that could be individually closed. Even if four or fewer consecutive compartments were breached, the ship could still stay afloat. Unfortunately, the glancing blow to an iceberg damaged five adjacent compartments, and over 1,600 souls lost their lives due to an insufficient number of seats in the Titanic's lifeboats.

So why wasn't there a place for each passenger and crew member on these secondary safety devices? The answer was that up until that time, the Merchant Shipping Act of 1894 required ships weighing more than 10,000 tons to only have 16 lifeboats. The Titanic weighed four times that and could have carried up to 64 lifeboats. Instead, it chose to be in technical compliance with this law of the sea by having 20 total boats. Fourteen of the boats could carry up to 65 people, but the first few launched after the iceberg strike carried far fewer than the maximum number allowed. Most lifeboats carried only women, children, and some wealthy men. The 20 boats could have accommodated 1,178 people, approximately one-third of the people aboard. There were several reasons for this strategy:

- It was almost unthinkable that the ship was sinkable. In case of an accident, designers thought the safest place would be on the ship.
- Ships had a new technology of Marconi wireless telegraphs that could communicate with the many other ships in the area. If a disaster occurred, the 20 lifeboats could make several trips to ferry the passengers and crew to ships coming to their aid.
- More than 20 lifeboats seemed to "clutter" the upper decks and obscure the view of high-paying first-class passengers.

Doing more than the minimal legal requirements and focusing on safety could have saved so many additional lives. Two years after the Titanic tragedy, the International Convention for the Safety of Life at Sea (SOLAS) required ships to have one lifeboat seat for every person on the ship.

### The Foreign Corrupt Practices Act

Another problem with strict constructionists deals with defining "the line." The same action might be above or below the mark, depending on what country, state, county, or city you're in, and even which judge is presiding over the issue.

The Foreign Corrupt Practices Act (FCPA) criminalizes bribes by those operating in the United States given to foreign officials to obtain new business or retain current contracts. This same law has a loophole which allows American businesspeople to avoid criminal liability if they give small "facilitating" or "grease payments" to border guards or customs officials. The only real difference between bribes to high-ranking foreign officials and low-level bureaucrats is the order of magnitude and whether new business is bought. Even though this might be a distinction without much of a difference, some shrug their shoulders, wink, and move on. It just seems easier to give a small payment to an underpaid, low-level customs official, than it is to refuse the "grease" and incur their wrath or apathy. American businesspeople with this mindset convince themselves they no longer have to fight for each cargo container waiting at the port to be processed and transported in-country. It's justified as a "tip" or "gratuity" for "concierge level service" to get paperwork from the bottom of the stack to the top of the pile. That same small facilitating payment by a British citizen or person doing business in Great Britain would violate the 2010 UK Bribery Act.

Recommendation

*Dancing this close to the line ("line dancing"?) is a dangerous practice, which can come with severe consequences. Values-based leaders should do more than "nano-compliance" by building an ethical buffer which protects both the individual and the company. Former U.S. Supreme Court Justice Potter Stewart stated, "Ethics is knowing the difference between what you have a right to do and what is right to do." In Jurassic Park, Dr. Ian Malcom (Jeff Goldblum) made a similar point by saying, "Your scientists were so preoccupied with whether they could that they didn't stop to think if they should."*

**Incrementalists—"Those Who Believe in or Advocate for Change By Degrees; Gradualism."**

## Case Study 3.3—The Story of the Christmas Ham

Philosopher Jonathan Glover described incrementalism as how "we slide into participation by imperceptible degrees so that there is never the sense of a frontier being crossed."[3] George Lefcoe, former LA County Regional Planning Commissioner and law professor at the University of Southern California, demonstrated this thought process and subtle changes behind sliding down the slippery slope. Upon the occasion of his retirement from public office, he made these comments about the perks and seduction of public life when he talked about "the Christmas Ham."[4]

My first Christmas as commissioner, I tried to return (the ham).
My guess is that not one of the many public servants who
received the ham ever had tried to return it.
*(Righteous Indignation)*
When I received another ham the next Christmas,
I gave it to a worthy charity.
*(Small Justification)*
The next year, some worthy friends were having a party,
so I gave it to them.
*(Defensible Explanation)*
The next year I had a party, and we enjoyed the ham.
*(Full Rationalization)*
In the fifth year, about the tenth of December,
I began wondering, where is my ham?
*(Outright Entitlement)*

Not many people start out at the "ham as a birthright" phase, and most don't jump from mild disgust directly to an expected perk of pork. Some proceed down the path, one baby step at a time, until they end at a place they never expected to reach. It's death by a thousand spiral cuts to both the ham and the conscience.

What goes through an employee's mind during this downward descent? Receiving a gift might seem legal, but should be disclosed, reported properly, and not accepted in anticipation of returning a favor (no quid pro quo—this for that). In many cultures, it might appear rude to refuse a small token of friendship and could end up costing the deal or the contribution. In Commissioner Lefcoe's first year of the "hamgate" incident, he wasn't sure whether accepting it was proper, but it seemed to bother him. What was Forest Lawn cemetery trying to do? Befriend him? Influence him? Buy him? For the cost of a ham? He could defend his initial action by giving the pesky porker away. It may have been inconvenient, but at least some needy people could benefit, and he would keep his integrity intact.

Another year. Another ham. Another explanation. This time, perhaps with some indigestion but without the side order of indignation. The smoked swine that initially left such a bad taste in his mouth was getting more and more palatable. Savory even. After just a few years, he started salivating in anticipation right after Thanksgiving. Slippery slope successfully slid. Now where's that carving knife?

### Slicing the Salami

Continuing with the concept of charcuterie, there is another incrementalism theory known as "salami slicing." It is defined as "a series of actions to remove or reduce something by small amounts over a period of time, so that people are less likely to notice any changes." Reflection is an important part of a Jesuit education, and a former student wrote this quote in her journal while discussing "slippery slopes."

> One other piece of discussion that was brought up in class is how, little by little, it's easy to go down a non-ethical path. At work, I call this "salami slicing." Say you have a [process that uses 10 percent of a material]. The company decides to cost-save the formula for a given reason, but we want to make sure the consumer still gets the benefit. We lower the [factor] to 9 percent. The formulas are compared, and no noticeable negatives are seen—management approves the 9 percent [factor]. A few months later, there is a need to cost save again, the same happens, the 9 percent [factor] is compared to the 8 percent, and no noticeable negatives are seen. As this happens over and over, you end up in a 5 percent [factor] thinking you are still good since you are "salami slicing" little by little. If you were to compare the 10 percent formula with the new 5 percent, I am sure the differences would be huge; yet, you blind yourself to think you are "still okay." It is interesting seeing that when a series of events happen gradually, it numbs the "ethical muscle" into believing it is okay. Every day we push boundaries, and we find ourselves in situations that are hard to assess.[5]

The thing that was once tolerable and maybe even legal now bears little resemblance to the original action. It has progressed from acceptable to unethical and possibly illegal, one small sliver at a time.

Former Harvard Business School professor, Clayton Christensen cautioned against the dangers associated with committing that first bad act:

> Behavioral ethics can warn people that they are subject to making these errors, just like everyone else, and therefore enable them to realize that they must take precautions. It can remind them that "the first dishonest act is the most important one to prevent." It can instill in them Clayton Christensen's lesson that it is easier to be ethical 100 percent of the time than 98 percent of the time, because that 2 percent leeway you give yourself becomes 3 percent and then 5 percent, and then 10 percent, and so on.[6]

What a great goal—to be ethical 100 percent of the time! Principled principals can encourage employees to mitigate these ethical slip-ups by having them write down on a paper slip, things they would never do. Examples could include—"I won't let a co-worker get blamed for my mistakes," or "I'll never backdate a deal," or "I'll never act in a way I couldn't explain to my young child or mother."

## Recommendation

*VBLs should caution their staff about starting down the slippery slope. Employees might struggle with their original decision, but after significant soul searching, reluctantly acquiesce to the "one time" request. To quote Cat Stevens, Rod Stewart, and Sheryl Crow—"the first cut is the deepest" and can lead to future sliding by pointing employees in the wrong direction. Unfortunately, once they've done that deed, it becomes increasingly difficult to refuse, and easier to accept, the second, fifth, and tenth requests. They no longer have the moral high ground, and it becomes tougher to reverse course.*

### Altruists—"Believers in or Practitioners of Disinterested and Selfless Concern for the Well-Being of Others."

While incrementalists may start above the line of the law, altruists typically operate somewhere below it. They just have different motivations and intentions than other lawbreakers. Behavioral Economist—Dan Ariely—explains how this operates:

> People are able to cheat more when they cheat for other people. In some experiments, people cheated the most when they didn't benefit at all. This makes sense if our ability to be dishonest is increased by the ability to rationalize our behavior. If you're cheating for the benefit of another entity, your ability to rationalize is enhanced. So yes, it's easier for an accountant to see fudging on clients' tax returns as something other than dishonesty. And it's a concern within companies, since people's altruistic tendencies allow them to cheat more when it benefits team members.[7]

VBLs may consider altruists as people who do selfless, as opposed to selfish, acts. Part of this can be due to how someone "frames" the issue. One way to think about "framing" is we would much rather eat a hamburger that was labeled "75 percent fat free" (yeah!), instead of one claiming to have "25 percent fat" (yuch!). An employee might justify breaking a rule or a law by considering themselves loyal, not corrupt. So how do managers view these good soldiers who "take *one for* the team?" Typically, better than the ones who "take *some from* the team." In 2007, retired New York Yankee pitcher Andy Pettitte demonstrated this when he confessed:

> I felt an obligation to get back to my team as soon as possible. For this reason, and only for this reason, for two days I tried human growth hormone (HGH) ... I wasn't looking for an edge. I was looking to heal.[8]

Mr. Pettitte took the HGH in 2002, which wasn't banned from baseball until 2005. While his intentions may have been good, his actions were questionable but not illegal at the time.

Altruists may convince themselves their main motivation is helping others, but pride, ego, and even narcissism can also factor into the equation. Some people can't tolerate being associated with a failed project or company. They might also be frustrated, believing the procedures are outdated, cumbersome, and ineffective. Why not just cut to the chase, ignore the rules, and give the company a benefit they didn't have before? Some believe it is easier to ask for forgiveness afterwards than to be denied permission beforehand, especially when the organization seems to come out ahead. Irrespective of whether their motives are pure or mixed, altruists appear loyal to others. Unfortunately, this loyalty is misguided, and their "gifts" to the company are tainted.

In the short term, altruists may break records (either sports, sales, productivity, or others), but at the end of the day, their achievements will be accompanied by an "*" after their dirty deeds are discovered and disclosed. Values-based leaders can't quietly scold the offending employee while accepting benefits from their improper actions. All this does is develop and deepen a corrupt corporate culture.

## Recommendation

*Altruists who believe that certain policies are inappropriate or simply wrong should come forward and publicly advocate for change. They shouldn't act secretly, justifying their improper action by believing they will benefit others. This public discourse allows principled principals to openly discuss concerns. VBLs may be convinced by the altruist's logic and then attempt to change the policy, regulation, or law. If the values-based leader disagrees, they can't just close their eyes to the violation and accept the benefits. VBLs may appreciate loyalty but must require integrity. Breaking the rules to help the company or the team is still breaking the rules. Altruists' improper actions may be understandable but cannot be acceptable.*

## Prisoners—"Those Who Feel Trapped or Confined by a Situation or Set of Circumstances."

There is an old story about a man who offended the king and was sentenced to death. This man pleaded with his royal highness, asking he be spared. He told the king, that given a year, he could teach the ruler's favorite horse to sing. If successful, he should be released. With failure, he would willingly go to the gallows. The king was both intrigued and amused (maybe he enjoyed the classic television show Mr. Ed and wanted a seranading stallion of his own), so he sent the prisoner to the stables on this mission. On his way to the barn, a guard questioned the inmate's sanity. The prisoner replied, "A lot can happen in a year. The king might die. I might die. The horse might die, and who knows—maybe the horse will learn to sing." Sometimes prisoners just want a little more time. Maybe they'll come up with a solution. Perhaps circumstances will change. At least they'll have another year.

Not all prisoners are as quick-witted as the would-be horse whisperer. Many feel trapped by circumstances beyond their control. In the 1998 movie *Snake Eyes* (directed by Brian DiPalma), Nicholas Cage plays the semicorrupt Atlantic City cop—Rick Santoro. Julia Costello (Carla Gugino) portrays a defense contractor turned whistleblower. She has just unburdened herself by telling Santoro his best friend—Commander Kevin Dunne (Gary Sinise)—was the leader in a conspiracy to murder the Secretary of Defense. The newly burdened Santoro shrieks in his best Nick Cage "crazy eyes," now "Snake Eyes" way,

> Because I didn't have to know! You decided to have this problem, not me! My world would've gone on turning just fine, but now, either way I look, I have to do something I don't wanna do. Do you understand, I do not wanna to do this![9]

Instead of being informed but conflicted, he wished he had stuck his fingers in his ears while screaming, "La, la, la, la, la. I can't hear you."

Perhaps politics can provide the answer to how prisoners should proceed. The 1973 Watergate hearings ran from dawn to dusk coverage and even pre-empted afternoon soap operas. Senator Howard Baker kept asking Nixon's aide, "What did the President know, and when did he know it?" Imagine being cross-examined by a zealous prosecutor, asking—"What did you know, and when did you know it?" The follow-up to this question might be, "What did you do, once you knew it?" Values-based leaders can be a tolerant bunch. They don't like mistakes, but over time, these can be forgiven. What do VBLs hate? Cover-ups! In an April 24, 2023 post on Twitter, motivational speaker Simon Sinek says, "Trust has two dimensions: competence and integrity. We will forgive mistakes of competence. Mistakes of integrity are harder to overcome."

Since the 1973 political conspiracy, there is a new shorthand way of describing this type of behavior. Just add the four letters … "gate" to the end of the scandal, and the subject becomes a prisoner to the headlines. At least for the next news cycle, or two.

Recommendation

*When someone is alerted to a potential problem, assume values-based leaders will also find out about it. An employee's initial response shouldn't be looking for excuses or blaming someone else. Maybe they can bury the problem—at least for the time being, but plausible deniability won't solve anything. These employees must investigate what happened and propose viable solutions to their VBLs. Associates who caused part of the problem should accept responsibility, apologize, and learn from it. They should be transparent and keep the company and the public informed about their actions. They need to explain why something happened and then what they are doing to make sure it doesn't happen again. Values-based leaders understand that even prisoners can be pardoned with time off for good behavior.*

### Browbeaten—"Those Who are Intimidated, Typically Into Doing Something, With Stern or Abusive Words."

**Jim Young (Ben Affleck) in "Boiler Room":** *[to the new recruits]* And there is no such thing as a no sale call. A sale is made on every call you make. Either you sell the client some stock or he sells you a reason he can't. Either way a sale is made, the only question is who is gonna close? You or him? Now be relentless, that's it, I'm done.[10]

Employers can use a variety of techniques to motivate employees. On the positive end of the spectrum are performance bonuses. The opposite could result in termination.

Compensation structures can have direct social and moral effects, which is why executive compensation is a critical corporate governance issue that must be overseen closely. Compensation structures that do not include an ethics component can encourage the wrong types of behavior. For example, a large pay increase that is tied to unreasonable performance targets could help an individual to rationalize unethical and excessive risk taking. Stock options, profit sharing, bonuses, executive retirement benefits, severance policies and other perks should be aligned with a corporate commitment to ethical behavior.[11]

## Case Study 3.4—Glengarry, Glen Ross

This "darker side" of driving bad behavior played out in the 1992 movie *Glengarry Glen Ross*. Alec Baldwin plays Blake, the top salesperson in a fictional real estate firm, who earned $970,000 in commissions the previous year. He takes no prisoners and believes "the sale *begins* when the customer says '*No*'." Blake's on a mission of mercy for his employers, Mitch and Murray, who have asked him to light a fire under the troops at the local office. Blake chastises Shelly "The Machine" Levine—(Jack Lemmon)— to "put that coffee down. Coffee is for closers only." Blake puts Dave Moss—(Ed Harris)—in his place by bragging that his watch costs more than Moss' car. The final act of motivation or humiliation occurs when Blake explains the new rules of the game.

> Cause we're adding a little something to this month's sales contest. As you all know first prize is a Cadillac El Dorado. Anyone wanna see second prize? Second prize is a set of steak knives. Third prize is you're fired.[12]

In this cutthroat, dog-eat-dog environment, people are under so much pressure they'll do anything to survive. They are desperate to get a promising lead, trying any tactics to convince one of their recycled cold-called prospects to agree to a "sit"—(a meeting in the customer's home)— so they can sell real estate, snake oil, widgets, or any other useless product at inflated prices.

The movie is shot in dark primary colors. Blurry blues and flashing reds set the scene for this primal battle. One's worth is measured by what they've done for the firm lately, not the nostalgic glory days of winning past contests. These salesmen eat what they kill, and their "cavemanhood" is continuously challenged. Baldwin's Blake is the consummate bully, and the rest of the office suffers his abuse. The one exception is Ricky Roma—(Al Pacino)—who is excused from the verbal beatdown because he is on the top of the Cadillac board and top of the world. Roma is absent because he is closing a new client, James Lingk—(played by Jonathan Pryce)—with big stories, false flattery, misdirection, lies, and seduction. Roma is the living embodiment of Blake's sales mantra—"A.B.C.—Always Be Closing." *Glengarry Glen Ross* exposes us to "duress for success." Do whatever it takes to "hit the numbers."

## Case Study 3.5—Wells Fargo

A real-life example of a high-pressure business is how Wells Fargo treated its employees from 2002 to 2016:

> In court papers, prosecutors described a pressure-cooker environment at the bank, where low-level employees were squeezed tighter and tighter each year by sales goals that senior executives methodically raised, ignoring signs that they were unrealistic. The few employees and managers who did meet sales goals—by any means—were held up as examples for the rest of the work force to follow.[13]

Bankers were pushed to cross-sell financial products and would engage in fraudulent schemes to fulfill its CEO—John Stumpf's—rallying cry of "eight is great." Wells Fargo customers with one account were encouraged to subscribe to other fee-generating products until the magic number of "eight" was met. If they didn't do it voluntarily, some Wells Fargo employees would open secret accounts for the clients and get the credit. Sometimes, these accounts would be cancelled by the Wells Fargo employee; other times, they went undetected until the customer received notices from bill collectors, negatively impacting their credit scores.

> "I had managers in my face yelling at me," Sabrina Bertrand, who worked as a licensed personal banker for Wells Fargo in Houston in 2013, told CNNMoney. "They wanted you to open up dual checking accounts for people that couldn't even manage their

original checking account." ... The pressure cooker environment is also described in a lawsuit filed by Los Angeles against Wells Fargo in May 2015. The lawsuit says that Wells Fargo's district managers discussed daily sales for each branch and employee "four times a day, at 11 am, 1 pm, 3 pm and 5 pm."[14]

Stumpf's 2016 started well when he was named CEO of the year by Morningstar. After the news broke about this scandal, in October of that same year, he was forced to leave Wells Fargo, banned from ever working at a bank again, and personally had to pay a $17.5 million fine. Combining John Stumpf's individual sanctions along with Wells Fargo's $3,000,000,000 in criminal and civil fines, maybe their motto should have been "one and done!"

Given enough pressure over time, nature turns coal into diamonds. Under the same conditions—pressure over time—good employees can have their souls first hardened, then deadened. These ugly gemstones may not cut glass but are impervious to chipping or feeling. Glengarry Glen-workers don't wake up engaged, champing at the bit for another day, another opportunity, another challenge. They are disengaged, counting down the minutes until the end of the day as soon as they walk into the office. Bullied by the Blake bosses of the world, they don't care about work anymore. There is no joy, just the constant pressure to perform. They need to be on top of the board to win the Cadillac—or at least continue their drudgery and get the steak knives.

Recommendation

*When some cynical businesspeople hear the "E"—(ethics)—word, they think you can't have both high ethical standards and high-performance expectations. This is a misperception about the value of values. To rebut it, values-based leaders need to provide their employees adequate resources to accomplish these goals but to do so in an ethical fashion. This can come in the form of S.M.A.R.T. goals, standing for:*

- *Specific;*
- *Measurable;*

- *Attainable;*
- *Relevant;*
- *Time-bound.*

*Georgia Power conducted an Ethical Culture Inventory and asked the respondents to evaluate whether the company was weak or strong regarding the following question. "Feasibility—Managers at all levels give employees sufficient time, budget, resources and authority to fulfill their responsibilities."[15] Without adequate resources, if managers tell associates to "just get it done, and I don't care how you do it," employees will interpret this as tacit, if not explicit, approval to cheat.*

*One example of principled principals providing adequate resources deals with the message United Parcel Service (UPS) sent to its staff about bribery. On-time deliveries are one of the most important performance metrics for its employees. Threatening to delay in-country access gives foreign customs officials additional leverage to pressure UPS employees to pay bribes. The company limits this threat in the following way:*

*The United Parcel Service exempts shipments held up by corrupt customs officials seeking bribes from counting against employees' performance objectives for on-time deliveries. This exemption sends a clear message: You will not have to compromise our ethics to meet your numbers. UPS employees trust that when ethical push comes up against corrupt shove, they have the backing of their managers and leaders to do the right thing. Managers, even powerful district managers, are summarily removed from their positions if they fail to support employees in doing the right thing.[16]*

*UPS's VBLs empowered its employees to follow their conscience along with the company code of conduct.*

*Given the right tools, aggressive but realistic S.M.A.R.T. goals can create a rich and competitive work environment. Many employees will accept the challenge, follow the rules, and have a better attitude and work product. If values-based leaders don't pressure them to cheat and browbeat them into submission every day, these employees can become hidden gems for the company.*

*Conformists—"Those Who Make Themselves in Harmony With (a pattern or example); Who Bring Themselves Into Conformity, Adapt Themselves."*

## Case Study 3.6—A Few Good Men

The movie *A Few Good Men* was first a play written by Aaron Sorkin in 1989. He based the idea on an incident his sister, a young military attorney, experienced earlier in her career. Sorkin adapted the play into the screenplay for the 1992 movie of the same name, directed by Rob Reiner. Tom Cruise plays Lt. Daniel Kaffee, the affable Navy JAG attorney known for negotiating sweet plea agreements for his military clientele while still having plenty of time to practice his softball swing. Cruise's Kaffee is selected to defend two Marines—Corporal Dawson and Private Downey, both accused of killing Private Willy Santiago during a hazing incident called a "Code Red." Kaffee is only one year out of law school, but during that time, "He's successfully plea bargained 44 cases in nine months."[17] His quick to settle philosophy is exactly why his bosses from "division" selected him over the brilliant but procedurally awkward Lt. Commander JoAnne Galloway—(Demi Moore)—to represent Dawson and Downey. The case was designed to be swept under the carpet and never see the inside of a courtroom.

If convicted, the two Marines faced life in prison at Leavenworth. The prosecuting attorney, Captain Ross—(Kevin Bacon)—started the sentencing sanctions at 22 years apiece, then quickly dropped it to 12. When Kaffee pushed back, Ross gave his best and final offer, a two-year prison term, and with good behavior, Dawson and Downey could be released after six months. Surprised but pleased with a sentence lasting shorter than a hockey season, Kaffee took the offer to his clients expecting a sigh of relief, a thank you, and maybe even a salute. Instead, Corporal Dawson refuses the deal, stating, "We did nothing wrong, sir. We did our job. If that has consequences, then I accept them. But I won't say I'm guilty, sir."[18] Without their admission of guilt, Kaffee was forced to use the "just following orders" defense, knowing "that didn't work for Calley at My Lai, an argument that didn't work for the Nazis at Nuremberg."[19] Cruise tries to defend his clients by implicating the head of the Guantanamo Cuba

Marine base, Colonel Nathan Jessep—(Jack Nicholson). This was "risky business" for Cruise because falsely accusing a superior officer could get Kaffee court-martialed to a place that didn't have a softball field. Kaffee needed Jessep to hang himself. Maybe he would do just that, if Cruise supplied enough rope, through dialogue like this:

*Col. Jessep*:    Have you ever spent time in an infantry unit, son?
*Kaffee*:    No sir.
*Col. Jessep*:    Ever served in a forward area?
*Kaffee*:    No sir.
*Col. Jessep*:    Ever put your life in another man's hands, ask him to put his life in yours?
*Kaffee*:    No sir.
*Col. Jessep*:    We follow orders, son. We follow orders or people die. It's that simple. Are we clear?
*Kaffee*:    Yes sir.
*Col. Jessep*:    Are we clear?
*Kaffee*:    Crystal.[20]

Following this exchange, the Colonel tells Kaffee that he gave an order that Private Santiago not be touched. He later testified that he directed Santiago be flown to the U.S. mainland because he was in "grave" danger—(is there any other kind?). Kaffee challenges these two inconsistencies, attempting to show perjury and, ultimately, Jessep's complicity.

If you gave the order that Santiago was not to be touched, and your orders are always followed, then why would Santiago be in danger? Why would it be necessary to transfer him? ... You made it clear just a moment ago that your men never take matters into their own hands. Your men follow orders or people die. So, Santiago shouldn't have been in any danger at all, should he have, Colonel?[21]

Cornered, but not contrite, Jessep contemptuously educates young Kaffee on the truth that he may or may not be able to handle. The Colonel's ego, coupled with his dogmatic need for respect for the chain of command and rule-following, led to his admission of ordering the "Code Red," which resulted in Santiago's death. It seems that even when people follow Colonel Jessep's commands, some innocent people die. How is that noose feeling Colonel? Is it tight enough? Do you need any more rope?

Upon enlisting in the military, soldiers like the fictional Downey and Dawson take a loyalty oath of obedience. So why doesn't the "I was just doing what I was told" defense work? Soldiers are duty bound to follow the orders of their superiors, but this "Nuremberg Defense" didn't save Nazi and SS officer—Adolf Eichmann—from being convicted and hanged for crimes against humanity and war crimes on May 31, 1962. While soldiers must obey legal orders, they can disobey illegal ones. Deciphering which is which can be the tough part.

## Case Study 3.7—The Milgram Experiment

About the same time as Eichmann's trial, in 1961, Stanley Milgram, a Yale psychologist, started exploring the question of why people follow authority, even considering unthinkable consequences. "He (Milgram) was seeking an answer to the pertinent question: 'Could it be that Eichmann and his million accomplices in the Holocaust were just following orders?'"[22] Milgram's controversial experiment used three people—"the experimenter," "the teacher," and "the learner." Both the experimenter and the learner were in cahoots, and the real test was to see how far "the teacher" would go if prodded by an experimenter in a white lab coat. The fake experiment had groups of two people chosen to participate. Allegedly, the two participants "randomly" selected a piece of paper, assigning whether they were the "teacher" or the "learner." Unbeknownst to the real subject, both sheets of paper said "teacher," but the stooge always claimed to be the learner. Let the phony experiment begin!

The bogus backstory about the alleged experiment supposedly tested whether increasing electric shocks could help people remember word pairings. Before the experiment started, the teacher was administered a low dose of electricity by a machine to feel it was real. After this, the learner was removed to another room, behind a barrier obstructing their view. With each wrong answer, the teacher was instructed by the experimenter to increase the voltage.

Conflict arises when the man receiving the shock begins to indicate he is experiencing discomfort. At 75 volts, the "learner" grunts. At 120 volts he complains verbally; at 150 he demands to be released from the experiment. His protests continue as the shocks escalate, growing increasingly vehement and emotional. At 285 volts his response can only be described as an agonized scream.[23]

As the learner's cries grew louder, many teachers tried to stop participating in the experiment. After each of the teachers' protests, the experimenter said these statements in the following order:

1. "Please continue."
2. "The experiment requires that you continue."
3. "It is absolutely essential that you continue."
4. "You have no other choice, you must go on."

In Milgram's first experiment, 65 percent (26 out of 40) blindly followed orders and were willing to administer a seemingly lethal 450-volt shock.

Soldiers, psychology subjects, and staff have faced the pressure to obey authority figures. So, how does the "I was just following orders" defense work with low and mid-level white-collar criminals? It is not an excuse, but may help as a strategy for better treatment when prosecutors use them as legal chum to catch bigger fish. When government attorneys just follow the trail of those just following the orders, they can eventually "trade up" to the senior executives who issued them. What's the prosecutorial motivation and reward? Another high-profile conviction. Another press conference. Another notch in the belt. Another promotion. Another day in the office.

Recommendation

*Almost everything values-based leaders need to know about conformists can be learned in a college PSYC 101 class. Along with Milgram, psychologists from A—(Asch) to Z— (Zimbardo) have studied the question of how "normal," "good" people can first have their judgment subordinated and then be persuaded to do unimaginable acts. While Milgram explored authority, Asch—(Milgram's mentor)—and Zimbardo examined the influence groups have on our behavior.*

*Most people try to avoid conflict. They like fitting in with the group and understand the need to follow orders. It may seem counterintuitive, but employees should be willing to stand out from the crowd. By offering diverse perspectives, their teams will be stronger and come to better solutions than they would from polite head nods from corporate toadies too afraid to speak their minds. Einstein recognized the danger of conformity in a July 8, 1901 statement to Jost Winteler, "Slavish obedience to authority is the greatest enemy of the truth."[24] This same sentiment is captured in the 20th-century bumper sticker or t-shirt—"Question Authority." This can be good advice, but it should be followed by, "Do it in a respectful way."*

### Rationalizers—"Those who Explain or Justify Behavior or Attitude to Themselves or Others With Plausible, but Specious Reasons."

In 2014, at the Grace Hopper Celebration of Women in Computing Conference, Microsoft CEO Satya Nadella was asked how the tech industry should respond to wage disparity based on gender. He said:

> It's not really about asking for a raise, but knowing and having faith that the system will give you the right raise.... That might be one of the additional superpowers that quite frankly, women who don't ask for raises have. Because that's good karma. It will come back.

The public response to this statement, especially at this conference, was predictable, negative, and swift. To limit his own bad karma, Nadella's reaction was a tweeted retraction.

Now imagine an employee gathering the courage to ask for that well-deserved raise. Unfortunately, their boss tells them there is a salary freeze, so no one at their level is getting an increase, even though they both suspect senior managers are getting theirs. The supervisor suggests a sneaky alternative. The employee should consider increasing their travel and entertainment—(T&E)—expense report by about $50 a week.

The company's per diem reimbursement system expects strict accuracy but is based on trust and allows employees to voucher meal expenses under $50 without receipts. The supervisor instructs the employee to "Pay for a hot dog and claim it was a steak. How are they going to know what you ate? But make sure you don't repeat exact numbers from week to week, because that could raise a red flag." The supervisor promises to sign off on the employee's T&E reports, so they will get the equivalent of a $2,500 raise—($50 per week for 50 weeks)—tax-free and clear, as long as they are not caught by the IRS, FBI, local police, or the company's internal auditors. The employee is reassured not to worry because it is a common practice and no one will ever find out. They might rationalize participating in this scheme by thinking, "Who am I to argue with my boss. Anyway, I deserve the money, and work as many hours as the CEO who's making hundreds of times my salary. The company's making so much money, they'll never miss it." In his September 27, 2006 Memorandum to Berkshire Hathaway Managers, Warren Buffett warned about this mindset saying, "[T]he five most dangerous words in business may be 'Everybody else is doing it.'" Values-based leaders need to understand that employee mindset and act accordingly to change it.

## Case Study 3.8—The Matrix Experiment

Dan Ariely is a behavioral economist and professor at Duke University. He has researched and written extensively on rationalization. Ariely tells a story about a little boy who got in trouble for stealing a pencil from another student. The boy's father was mortified by the incident and told his son, "Johnny, that's terrible, you never steal, and besides if you need a pencil, let me know and I'll bring you a box from the office."[25] Behavior is learned by modeling different roles, including our parents, colleagues, and leaders.

Ariely researched these excuses by exploring how people can cheat and still consider themselves to be a "good person." His "Matrix" experiments involved distributing 20 sets of sheets, each one containing a series of different math questions to participants. They had a limited time to solve the problems and were awarded $1.00 for each correct answer. In the controlled format, when the test was monitored and responses could be confirmed, the average number of correct answers reported was four solutions in five minutes. In a second version, participants were allowed to take the test, shred their answers, declare to the proctor how many equations they solved correctly, and then collect their reward. What the participants didn't know was that only the edges of their answer sheets were shredded. After the participants left the room, the researchers could compare the number of correct answers declared with the actual results.

Ariely discovered there could be some significant financial implications for just cheating a little. In the uncontrolled experiment, he found that there was a small percentage of people who never lied, always answering the test honestly. He didn't lose any money on them. There was another small group that lied almost all the time, significantly inflating the number of their correct answers. While the experimenter lost more money per person, there weren't many who fell into this category, therefore not much money was lost in total. The surprising part was that the biggest loss came from those who only cheated a little. They may have solved four problems but reported five or six.

> Across all of our experiments, we've tested maybe 30,000 people, and we had a dozen or so bad apples and they stole about $150 from us. And we had about 18,000 little rotten apples, each of them just stole a couple of dollars, but together it was $36,000. And if you think about it, I think it's actually a good reflection of what happens in society.[26]

By just cheating a little, they could continue to consider themselves to be relatively honest and still a "good person." Ariely called this the "fudge factor."

In a way, this might be like speeding on the highway. Most people would never drive 90 on a highway zoned for 65 mph. Anyone who does that is reckless. They deserve at least a speeding ticket and maybe should have their license revoked. But what about traveling on that same interstate road at 66, 68, or even 72 mph? As drivers are gently pushing the accelerator pedal, they still consider themselves both good drivers and good people by rationalizing that they are just going the speed of traffic. This driver is certainly not as bad as the people who are passing them. In fact, they convince themselves that if they only drove 65 mph, they might create a dangerous condition by going too slow. Try explaining that logic to the Traffic-Cam that just clocked them going 72 in a 65-mph zone. One might consider themselves to be a "good person," but they will still have the points added onto their license and must pay the fine out of their own pocket. Like Ariely's math test takers, a little cheating or speeding may seem justifiable in their own minds but probably not to auditors, regulators, police, or cameras mounted on poles at the bottom of steep hills.

Recommendation

*Unfortunately, sometimes, these schemes are part of the company's corporate culture, passed down from previous generations of supervisors. Todd Haugh—Business Law and Ethics Professor at Indiana University—wrote on Linkedin:*

> *Employees don't conjure up the "fake it till you make it" mentality and resulting fraudulent behaviors out of thin air. They are taught it by people in your organization—sometimes the sales chief and sometimes their closest co-workers—and then they teach others. To stop wrongdoing in your company you have to stop this criminogenic learning cycle.[27]*

*Principled principals need to understand and deal with the root causes of their employee's rationalizations. Are they paying their employees a fair and living wage? If so, employees may still be unhappy, but they shouldn't use that as a justification for stealing from the company because it seems like "everybody else is doing it." Values-based leaders need to establish appropriate internal controls to prevent and detect violations for those "who do it anyway." VBLs should explain that employees can't just steal a little and still consider themselves good employees. They should consider themselves thieves and cheaters.*

*Hedonists—"Those Who Regard Pleasure as the Chief Good."*

## Case Study 3.9—Martha Stewart

"Why do talented, bright, highly educated, successful people, who have 'made it,' risk it all by lying, stealing and cheating, especially when what they're stealing is insignificant compared to what they have? The simple answer is, 'because they can.'"[28] This quote could have been applied to Martha Stewart's sale of her ImClone stock on December 27, 2001, the day before the FDA denied that company's request to have its drug—Erbitux—approved to treat cancer. ImClone's CEO was Sam Waksal. He and Ms. Stewart were friends and even bought and sold stock through the same firm. The day before the FDA announced it wouldn't approve Erbitux as a cancer treatment, Waksal somehow found out. He instructed his stockbroker to sell all his ImClone stock. Someone at that brokerage leaked the information to Martha Stewart, who also instructed them to sell her ImClone stock.

By selling her 3,928 shares of ImClone stock the day before the FDA publicly released its Erbitux decision, Martha Stewart avoided losses of $45,673. Losing $46,000 to Martha Stewart is a rounding error! It is a couple of New York City galas with fancy dresses and Jimmy Choo shoes. This would be equivalent to mid-level managers risking their reputation for the price of a mid-level Apple watch. No one likes losing money, but we shouldn't risk jail time for the financial equivalent of 500 bucks.

By the way, Martha Stewart was never convicted of insider trading, which can be difficult to prove. Instead, she was sentenced to five months in "Camp Cupcake,"—a minimum-security women's work camp in Alderson, West Virginia—on four counts of "obstruction of justice and lying to investigators" (a much easier case to make). Ms. Stewart didn't appeal her sentence, and she "did her time well." Since her release on March 5, 2005, Martha Stewart has done a wonderful job rehabilitating both her reputation and her brand. For all the customers and stakeholders associated with her company—Martha Stewart Living Omnimedia—that is "a good thing."

What did Pete Rose, Wesley Snipes, Al Capone, and Leona Helmsley have in common? They all went to prison for tax evasion. During Helmsley's trial, a former housekeeper testified that she overheard Leona saying, "We don't pay taxes. Only the little people pay taxes." Why do some rich and powerful people think the rules don't apply to them? What is the cause of this hubris? Sometimes it is because nobody told them to stop.

Around 1800, John Randolph had this description of Representative Edward Livingston of New York—"He is a man of splendid abilities but utterly corrupt. He shines and stinks like rotten mackerel by moonlight." Managers can't be dazzled by the numbers—(the shine)—delivered by high performers who get results but do it the wrong way—(the stink). To paraphrase Leona Helmsley, "Only the little people will follow policies."

## Recommendations

*Values-based leaders need to constantly remind, reinforce, and even "nudge" employees that no one is above the law or the company's code of ethics. Robert Prentice—Professor of Business Law and Business Ethics at the University of Texas at Austin—wrote:*

> *It should be the moral responsibility of ... every individual, to keep ethical considerations in his or her own frame of reference whenever making decisions. And it is the responsibility of firms that wish their employees to act legally and ethically to continually prompt them to do so. The behavioral ethics literature indicates that this can have a meaningful impact.*[29]

# Conclusion

There are many explanations about why good people can get lost in the Bermuda Triangle of misconduct. Some attempt to follow the line of the law as closely as possible—(strict constructionists). Others may start above the law but slowly dip below it—(incrementalists). Another group may be well-intentioned, putting their organization above their personal interests—(altruists). Others may feel trapped—(prisoners), pressured—(browbeaten), group followers—(conformists), or just convince themselves they can cheat a little bit and still be a good person—(rationalizers). The last group of people, like smelly dead mackerels, are just rotten—(hedonists).

# LESSON 4

# What to Do When Someone Finds Problems at Work?

The previous chapter discussed how values-based leaders can identify bad behavior and how to prevent it. This chapter explores how VBLs should create an environment in which employees can report internally, and how to deal with them once they raise their concerns. If employees go directly to an outside agency or the news, the question VBLs need to answer is, "Why didn't the reporter trust me to deal with their complaints?"

Principled principals doing business in the United States and Europe should understand the history of whistleblowing in both regions. Americans promoted whistleblower protection during the Revolutionary and Civil Wars and developed a bounty system to encourage employees to report government graft. When the United States is alerted about fraud and claws back the ill-gotten gains from violators, it is willing to share up to 30 percent of these proceeds with the reporters—(known as "relators").

Two of the biggest fears whistleblowers have are:

1. Retaliation;
2. Inaction.

Several U.S. laws promote whistleblowing hotlines and provide rewards and antiretaliation protection for reporters:

- Federal Sentencing Guidelines for Organizations;
- Sarbanes-Oxley;
- Dodd-Frank.

These laws are compared to Europeans regulations including:

- EU Whistleblower Protection Directive;
- UK's Public Interest Disclosure Act (PIDA).

This section includes case studies about whistleblowers like Frances Haugen (Facebook), Cynthia Cooper (WorldCom), Sherron Watkins (Enron), Coleen Rowley (FBI), Walter Tamosaitis (Energy Company), Roger Boisjoly (Space Shuttle Challenger), and Michael Woodford (Olympus). The chapter concludes by discussing what is happening inside the mind of the whistleblowers in deciding whether to come forward. After the whistleblowers become aware of a potential problem, do they know how to report it? Has the principled principal done a good job communicating how to disclose the information internally? How can VBLs convince whistleblowers to speak up? It is important for principled principals to listen and then follow up with appropriate action.

# #4—Snitches Get Stitches

## Introduction

"Rat on your pop, and Keyser Söze will get you." This was the children's bedtime warning, repeated in the movie *The Usual Suspects*. Söze sounds like a nightmarish Turkish composite of Freddy Krueger and The Godfather's Don Corleone. He might follow up with a menacing whisper—"Now, go to bed, and by the way—sweet dreams kiddies!" We get a similar sentiment with synonyms associated with blowing the whistle. Merriam Webster's Online Thesaurus lists words like "betrayer," "canary," "deep throat," "fink," "informant," "informer," "narc," "rat," "ratfink," "snitch," "snitcher," "squealer," "stool pigeon," "stoolie," "tattler," and "tattletale." These all seem to paint the reporter as a disgruntled employee looking for revenge, a payday, or maybe both. One rarely hears praise for the "loyal employee," "employee with a conscience," or "corporate hero" who surfaced potential problems. Is it because even if this is the right thing to do, it is going to cause plenty of extra work and headaches?

While the concept of whistleblowing has been around for centuries, in 1971, Ralph Nader defined it as—"an act of a man or woman who, believing that the public interest overrides the interest of the organization he (or she) serves, blows the whistle that the organization is involved in corrupt, illegal, fraudulent or harmful activity." This definition sets up the potential conflict between loyalty to one's organization and the duty to act in the public interest. Philosopher and ethicist—Sissela Bok—recognized this tension:

> ... a would-be whistleblower must weigh his (or her) responsibility to serve the public interest against the responsibility he (or she) owes to his (or her) colleagues and the institution in which he (or she) works" and "that [when] their duty [to whistleblow] so overrides loyalties to colleagues and institutions, they [whistleblowers] often have reason to fear the results of carrying out such a duty.[1]

Not every scholar agreed with Bok's position that blowing the whistle placed reporters at odds with their duty of loyalty. University of New Brunswick philosophy professor—Robert Larmer—wrote:

> ...the great majority of corporate whistleblowers ... [consider] themselves to be very loyal employees who ...[try] to use "direct voice" (internal whistleblowing), ... [are] rebuffed and punished for this, and then ... [use] "indirect voice" (external whistleblowing). They ... [believe] initially that they ... [are] behaving in a loyal manner, helping their employers by calling top management's attention to practices that could eventually get the firm in trouble.[2]

Larmer holds that telling an organization or co-worker about actual, potential, or perceived misconduct can square with loyalty—maybe even friendship. Frances Haugen—a former product manager at Facebook—demonstrated these two concepts could coexist. She became frustrated with the "company's lack of openness about its platforms' potential for harm and unwillingness to address its flaws."[3] On her last day of work, she explained her motives for going public with her concerns. "'I don't hate Facebook,' she wrote. 'I love Facebook. I want to save it.'"[4]

If a company or individual wasn't aware of the depth of their problem(s), alerting them provides an opportunity to reverse course, or at least not let things fester and get worse. If they did know about the legal or ethical ramifications of their misconduct, confronting them pops the wrongdoer's thought bubble that no one will ever find out. Once concealed, but now revealed, the accused must decide how to deal with this damaging information.

## The History of Whistleblowing

In 695 England, King Wihthred of Kent incentivized residents to report their neighbors who worked during the "forbidden time"—the Sabbath. That act was punishable by being locked up and displayed in the local stocks. To avoid this public humiliation (not to mention being pummeled with rotting fruit and vegetables)—violators could pay a fine called a *healsfang*, the medieval equivalent of a "get out of the pillory for a price" card. The reporter could collect 50 percent of the fine plus any profits the violator earned from their labor instead of worshipping during that forbidden time in question. This turns the phrase—"there is no rest for the wicked"—into —"if you don't rest—you're wicked!"

### An Independent Idea

One of the earliest cases of whistleblower protection in the United States happened during the Revolutionary War. In 1775, Commodore Esek Hopkins was named the first Commander in Chief of the Continental Navy. In 1777, after Commodore Hopkins intentionally countermanded Congressional orders, 10 of his officers petitioned the government to relieve Hopkins of his command. They cited his contemptuous behavior, along with torturing British prisoners. Hopkins dismissed two of the complainants—Richard Marven and Samuel Shaw—from the Navy. They were charged with criminal libel in a Rhode Island Court and jailed. Marven and Shaw brought this to the government's attention. Aghast, Congress had both released from prison and agreed to pay their legal fees of $1,418 (equivalent to about $50,000 in today's dollars). In addition, Congress passed a law stating it was:

> ...the duty of all persons in the service of the United States to give the earliest information to Congress or any other proper authority of any misconduct, frauds or misdemeanors committed by any officers or persons in the service of these states, which may come to their knowledge.[5]

Fourscore and six years later, Abraham Lincoln and Congress would revisit whistleblower laws and incentives.

### The War Between the States

"A jobber from Vermont, Jim Fisk, twisted his swagger mustache and grinned with a cock of his eye, 'You can sell anything to the government at almost any price you've got the guts to ask.'"[6] This was the corrupt mindset of many federal contractors during the Civil War. At this time of scarcity, fraud ran rampant, and army soldiers from the North discovered they needed actual gunpowder to fire bullets—not the sawdust contained in the otherwise empty wooden crates delivered to their front lines. Another example of this gutsy behavior was when Brooks Brothers sold uniforms to Yankee soldiers. Instead of using wool, these tailors glued together shredded, decaying rags and pressed them into something loosely resembling cloth. This composite material was called "shoddy." Unfortunately, it did not stand up to bad weather, and Union soldiers could wind up in their Union suits during the first heavy rain. The New York legislature spent $45,000 to replace these outfits—(worth approximately $10.8 million in present-day dollars). Since this incident, the word "shoddy" morphed from a noun describing poor-quality fabric to an adjective describing items "badly made or done."

## Laws Helping Whistleblowers

### The False Claims Act

Before 1870, there was no Department of Justice—(DoJ)—or Attorney General to prosecute graft against the government. So how could the United States try to claw back funds from fraudsters? One method was incentivizing citizens to act as "private attorneys general" to advance these cases and combat fraud, waste, and abuse. This concept was codified when President Lincoln pushed Congress to pass the "False Claims Act," which it did on March 2, 1863. This "Lincoln Law" included a bounty provision known as a *Qui Tam* award. *Qui Tam* was an abbreviation for "*Qui tam pro domino rege quam pro se ipso in hac parte sequitur*," which in English translates into "who sues in this matter for the king as well as for himself." Those reporting became known as "relators," and they were originally entitled to 50 percent of the amount recovered by the government, based on new information Washington didn't previously know. Even if the government gave away half of the judgment, it was still ahead in the game. First, the Treasury was collecting some money back from the fraudulent activity, fraud they might never have discovered but for the information provided by the relator. Second, potential fraudsters might be discouraged from even considering the misconduct based on the financial incentives to those who know—(relators)—getting the information to those who could do something about it—(the government).

One question posed early in the legislative process asked whether relators could still qualify for the bounty if they were somehow involved in the illegal activity. An original sponsor of the False Claims Act—Senator Jacob Howard—addressed this by stating:

> In short, sir, I have based the fourth, fifth, sixth, and seventh sections upon the old-fashion idea of holding out a temptation, and "setting a rogue to catch a rogue," which is the safest and most expeditious way I have ever discovered of bringing rogues to justice.[7]

Apparently, bad acts and bad actors could be excused if the government got something out of it.

The False Claims Act changed between 1863 and the present, with substantial modifications in 1986. These changes were enacted to combat losses that were estimated at about 10 percent of the annual federal budget due to fraud, waste, and abuse. Relators can now collect between 15 and 25 percent of the recovery if the government intervenes and uses its substantial resources to prosecute the fraud. This range increases from 15 to 30 percent if the government doesn't get involved and relators litigate the case themselves.

Values-based leaders of defense contractors and health care providers should pay particular attention to these laws because these two industries have been involved in some of the biggest government frauds. When the military pays $600 apiece for a toilet seat, or Medicare reimburses a hospital $20 for one generic aspirin, we see why Washington can use all the help it can get. In the 35 years between 1986 and 2021, settlements and judgments collected by the U.S. government exceeded $70 billion, with $5.6 billion in fiscal year 2021 alone.

### The Federal Sentencing Guidelines for Organizations

(For an in-depth analysis of the Federal Sentencing Guidelines for Organizations, please view Lesson 5—What Happens if a Leader's Company Gets in Trouble?)

In 1991, the United States Sentencing Commission—(USSC)—described the seven minimum requirements of an effective ethics and compliance program for organizations. One provision—§8B2.1(b)(5)—states that:

> the organization shall take reasonable steps (C) to have and publicize a system, which may include mechanisms that allow for anonymity or confidentiality, whereby the organization's employees and agents may report or seek guidance regarding potential or actual criminal conduct without fear or retaliation.

The USSC recognized that there could be different legal ramifications depending on whether the report was "anonymous" or "confidential." Imagine a stressed-out employee coming into their supervisor's office exclaiming, "I have a big problem, but you can't do anything about it." At this point, their boss should stop them explaining, "I can't promise not to do anything about it. In fact, it's most likely I will need to act on your information." The employee might then ask, "Well, can you at least keep it between us and protect my identity?" The response needs to be,

> I'll do everything possible to keep your name out of it, but if we're sued by a third party, or the government conducts an investigation asking who made this report, I have to give you up in a heartbeat.

Since we know the reporter's identity, the "... basic rule of discovery is that a party may obtain any information that pertains—even slightly—to any issue in the lawsuit, as long as the information is not 'privileged' or otherwise legally protected."[8]

"Anonymous reporting" means just that—unknown. So, when a company is being investigated or sued, and the opposing party wants to discover where certain information came from—the targeted organization can honestly answer, "we don't know who filed the complaint." Even though anonymous reporters may want to share their stories with others, they should resist the temptation in order to maximize their protection. Lizl Groenewald—Senior Manager at the Ethics Institute— wrote:

> If you decide to speak up anonymously, do not, under any cir-
> cumstances, tell anyone (e.g., colleagues, family, friends, pastor)
> that you have done so. Blowing the whistle anonymously means
> that you report misconduct without providing any details about
> yourself. Keep it that way.[9]

In the nine years between the Federal Sentencing Guidelines for Organizations enactment and Y2K (1991–2000), rampant company failures provided another legislative opportunity to protect whistleblowers.

## Case Study 4.1—2002 Time People of the Year and Sarbanes-Oxley

Omertà is a blood oath, used by the Mafia to ensure secrecy and protect the group. While businesspeople may not suffer the same initiation rituals, organizations can also be protective of their dirty secrets. Who would be willing to leave the corporate cone of silence and violate the corporate code of silence, risking all the negative consequences? As the dot.com bubble burst at the beginning of the 21st century, that question was answered when Sherron Watkins—(Enron)—and Cynthia Cooper—(WorldCom)—reported accounting irregularities within their companies. Their revelations ultimately led to the collapse of their respective organizations. On December 2, 2001, even with $63.4 billion in assets, Enron sought Chapter 11 protection, creating the largest U.S. bankruptcy filing in history. Not to be outdone, on July 21, 2002, WorldCom filed for similar protection, but it had $107 billion in assets. This new American record for the biggest bankruptcy lasted until the 2008 failures of Washington Mutual ($327 billion in assets) and Lehman Brothers ($691 billion in assets).

Businesses aren't the only entities with secrets. The government also has its fair share. Coleen Rowley was an FBI agent working in their Minneapolis field office. In mid-August 2001, she obtained credible evidence about a possible attack being coordinated by Zacarias Moussaoui, one of the masterminds behind 9/11.

> Already deemed a potential terrorist threat, Moussaoui remained in custody due to a lapsed visa as Rowley's team, collaborating with the French Intelligence Service, confirmed within days his connections to radical fundamentalist Islamic groups and to Osama bin Laden. Even with this knowledge, the FBI denied Rowley a warrant to search Moussaoui's computer for information until the day of the attacks.[10]

In May 2002, Rowley sent a 13-page letter to the FBI Director Robert Mueller exposing Washington's inaction.

So, what impact did doing the right thing have on these three women?

> Their lives may not have been at stake, but Watkins, Rowley and Cooper put pretty much everything else on the line. Their jobs, their health, their privacy, their sanity—they risked all of them to bring us badly needed word of trouble inside crucial institutions.[11]

This trio changed the perception of whistleblowers as "narcs" to "heroes" and were celebrated as the 2002 Time Magazine Persons of the Year. This praise didn't sit well with all Time awardees. As an internal auditor for WorldCom, Cynthia "Cooper could not stomach the attention. 'I'm not a hero. I'm just doing my job,' she said. 'There was nothing to celebrate,' she remembers."[12]

It was time for new legislation protecting anyone brave enough to follow in the footsteps of Watkins, Cooper, and Rowley. Senator Paul Sarbanes—(Democrat from Maryland)—and Representative Michael Oxley—(Republican from Ohio)—cosponsored bipartisan legislation, reacting:

> ...to these scandals by enacting the Sarbanes-Oxley Bill in 2002, which has perhaps the strongest whistleblower protection rules in the world. It includes safeguards against discrimination at work,

establishes procedures to make disclosures more feasible and abolishes the organisational code of silence that normally prevented full disclosure.[13]

The Sarbanes-Oxley Act contains three sections specifically dealing with whistleblowers: §§806, 1107, and 301. Section 806 protects employees of publicly traded companies who report problems internally from being fired. If an employee believes their employer retaliated against them, they have 180 days to file a complaint with the U.S. Secretary of Labor. Employers who knowingly violate §806 are required to make the whistleblower whole. This includes reinstatement to a similar seniority position the employee would have had except for the discrimination, along with back pay with interest and litigation costs, including attorney's fees.

Even before Sarbanes-Oxley passed, Federal law protected witnesses against threats of violence. Section 1107 of Sarbanes-Oxley expanded this provision to include negative employment actions against cooperating witnesses.

> Whoever knowingly, with the intent to retaliate, takes any action harmful to any person, including interference with the lawful employment or livelihood of any person, for providing to a law enforcement officer any truthful information relating to the commission or possible commission of any Federal offense, shall be fined under this title or imprisoned not more than 10 years, or both.[14]

A prosecutor would need to prove: (1) the employer intended to retaliate, and (2) the whistleblower provided law enforcement with truthful information about the commission of a federal offense. This new breed of corporate Kaiser Söze's now faces up to a decade in federal prison for exacting vengeance against anyone who exposed them.

Section 301 of Sarbanes-Oxley holds that publicly traded companies must have their audit committees establish a confidential mechanism for receiving complaints about accounting irregularities. Reporting potential fraud directly to the board can be crucial, especially if senior management is somehow complicit in the misconduct. How else can the board exercise its duty to govern and oversee operations?

Almost immediately after its passage, some proclaimed Sarbanes-Oxley whistleblower protections would be a "game changer." American University Washington College of Law Professor—Robert Vaughn—wrote, "Indeed, because of its scope and its likely extraterritorial application, it may be the most important whistleblower protection law in the world." Taxpayers Against Fraud believed the law was "the single most effective measure possible to prevent recurrences of the Enron debacle and similar threats to the nation's financial markets."[15] Unfortunately, Sarbanes-Oxley whistleblower protection didn't live up to this hype.

> Yet, in the first three years after the statute's enactment, the Act failed to protect the vast majority of employees who filed Sarbanes-Oxley retaliation claims. During this time, 491 employees filed Sarbanes-Oxley complaints with the Occupational Safety and Health Administration (OSHA), the agency charged with initially investigating such complaints. OSHA resolved 361 of these cases and found for employees only 13 times, a win rate of 3.6 percent. On appeal from 93 OSHA decisions, administrative law judges (ALJs) in the Department of Labor found in favor of 6 employees, a win rate of 6.5 percent.[16]

About the same time as the dot.com failures, another business sector was on the verge of collapsing. This would create the next financial crisis and regulatory response.

### Dodd-Frank Wall Street Reform and Consumer Protection Act (Dodd-Frank)

In the early 2000s, banks flooded the housing market with easy money for buyers, regardless of their credit scores. "Morgenson and Rosner quote one Countrywide executive concerning its lending strategy: 'The sole criterion used to determine whether an applicant got a loan, he explained, was if a person could fog a mirror.'"[17] Another example of Countrywide's permissive lending strategy was retold by Michael

Winston, who in 2006 was an executive vice president in the company's leadership development area:

> He (Winston) found himself parked next to a man in the Countrywide lot whose car had vanity plates that read, "Fund'Em."
>
> "I said: 'I'm not familiar with that expression. What is this about?'" Mr. Winston recalled. The man replied that the term described the company's growth strategy for 2006 to fund all loans.
>
> "I was brand new and I said, 'What if the person has no job?'" Mr. Winston said.
>
> The answer: "Fund 'em."
>
> "What if the person has no assets?"
>
> Again: "Fund 'em."[18]

Countrywide and other lenders appeared to be modern-day alchemists, transmuting lead (bundled high-risk subprime mortgages) by sprinkling financial fairy dust on it, and voila—we now have gold—(AAA-rated mortgage-backed securities). No Income, no Job, no Assets—NINJA—loans were no problem, especially as adjustable-rate mortgages. This debt would start with affordable low-interest teaser rates, then the balloon payments would increase dramatically after a few years. Lenders told borrowers not to worry about the heightened future payments because their houses would quickly appreciate, enough to refinance the loan at a more favorable rate. If nothing else, owners could sell their property and cash out the built-up equity for a profit. That calculation only works in a market where housing prices go in one direction—up. This didn't account for widespread defaults when owners who were "underwater" in their equity just walked away from the homes.

> From the mortgage originator, to the loan servicer, to the mortgage-backed security issuer, to the CDO issuer, to the CDS protection seller, to the credit rating agencies, and to the holders of all those securities, at no point did any institution stop the party or question the little-understood computer risk models, or the blatantly unsustainable deterioration of the loan terms of the underlying mortgages.[19]

In 2008, the housing market collapsed quicker than Jared Vennett's—(Ryan Gosling)— Jenga tower in the movie *The Big Short*. All the greed—along with the "mirror fogging" and "Fund 'em" lending mentality—led to credit markets being frozen. This caused Countrywide and other venerable Wall Street banks like Lehman Brothers and Bear Stearns to fail. The Dodd-Frank Wall Street Reform and Consumer Protection Act was enacted in 2010 to address many of the issues that gave rise to the mortgage meltdown, incorporating expanded whistleblowing protections.

> Included (in Dodd-Frank) is legislation to support whistleblowers, as it became apparent that many insiders in the financial industry were well aware of excessive risk-taking by banking institutions and other financial giants and that fraudulent activity, insider trading, Ponzi schemes, and other criminal acts were occurring. The failure of individuals to step forward to report the wrongdoing was the consequence of hostile work environments that do not tolerate naysayers in the face of potential monumental profits.[20]

The False Claims Act offers whistleblowers bounties, and Sarbanes-Oxley promises them protection against retaliation. Section 922 of Dodd-Frank would combine both strategies.

### Section 922

Sections 922(b)(1)(A) and (B) of Dodd-Frank awards between 10 and 30 percent of the amount collected by the government, based on new information provided by the whistleblower that results in "monetary sanctions exceeding $1,000,000." In 2020, the SEC adopted amendments that:

> ...provide a mechanism for whistleblowers with potential awards of less than $5 million (which historically have represented nearly 75 percent of all whistleblower awards), subject to certain criteria, to qualify for a presumption that they will receive the maximum statutory award amount. Other awards will continue to be evaluated consistent with past practice.[21]

For awards potentially larger than $5,000,000, factors the SEC will consider that would increase the percentage include: (1) how significant was the information, and (2) how much assistance the whistleblower provided.[22]

To facilitate reporting misconduct, the SEC established "a separate office within the Commission to administer and enforce the provisions of section 21F of the Securities Act of 1934." In 2012, the SEC established the Office of the Whistleblower to carry out these duties, and it successfully incentivized people to come forward with complaints. As of 2021, the

> ...SEC has awarded approximately $1 billion to 207 individuals since issuing its first award in 2012. All payments are made out of an investor protection fund established by Congress that is financed entirely through monetary sanctions paid to the SEC by securities law violators. No money has been taken or withheld from harmed investors to pay whistleblower awards. Whistleblowers may be eligible for an award when they voluntarily provide the SEC with original, timely, and credible information that leads to a successful enforcement action. Whistleblower awards can range from 10-30 percent of the money collected when the monetary sanctions exceed $1 million.[23]

Section 806 of the Sarbanes-Oxley Act allowed whistleblowers who suffered retaliation to receive their back pay, with interest, along with reasonable attorneys' fees. Section 922(h)(1)(C)(ii) of Dodd-Frank doubles this antiretaliation protection, providing relief—"2 times the amount of back pay otherwise owed to the individual; and (iii) compensation for litigation costs, expert witness fees, and reasonable attorneys' fees."

## Case Study 4.2—*Digital Realty v. Somers*

One important question regarding the bounty and antiretaliation provisions of Dodd-Frank was, could a person qualify for either if they only reported their concerns internally and not to the SEC? Those were the facts facing Paul Somers, the vice president of Digital Realty Trust from 2010 to 2014. Somers was fired by his employer shortly after he reported violations to senior managers at his company. The bounty provision of Dodd-Frank—§922(a)(6)—states the "term 'whistleblower' means any individual who provides, or 2 or more individuals acting jointly who provide, information relating to a violation of the securities laws to the Commission, in a manner established, by rule or regulation, by the Commission." Since Mr. Somers only reported internally, it was clear he wouldn't qualify for a reward under that section. But what about §922(h) and its antiretaliation protection? Could Somers still seek twice his back pay? Both Somers and the SEC thought the answer was yes.

Somers argued for a bifurcated system that would allow one definition of whistleblower under §922(a)—requiring reporting to the SEC for a reward, and an expanded definition under §922(h) for antiretaliation protection that would also include those who only complained internally. In a 9-0 decision written by Associate Justice Ginsburg, the Supreme Court disagreed with the SEC's "dual structure" argument and ruled against Somers. It held that the whistleblower definition in §922(a)(6) applied to both remedies. Somers couldn't even receive one-time back pay under Sarbanes-Oxley §806 because he didn't file a complaint with the Department of Labor within that law's 180-day statute of limitations.

This strict reading of Dodd-Frank could lead to some unintended consequences. Many values-based leaders spend significant sums developing, staffing and investigating complaints filed using the company's "hotline," "help line," "open talk," or "speak up" line. Principled principals want employees to report internally first, giving supervisors and managers a chance to find and fix the problems before the outside world gets involved. After the Somers decision, it wouldn't be surprising if whistleblowers skipped internal reporting altogether and reported directly to the SEC. That way, they would qualify for the bounty, plus receive job protection under Dodd-Frank. Employees may fear that if they file their complaints internally first, they might be fired on the spot, immediately escorted out of the building by security, and have their proof confiscated and destroyed. To protect this type of information, whistleblowers should make backup copies of their evidence and store this information privately, not on company premises or property.

## McDonald's in France

In the 1994 movie—*Pulp Fiction*—Vincent—(John Travolta)—explains to Jules—(Samuel L. Jackson)—the difference between a French and American McDonald's.

> Jules:    "What do they (the French) call a Big Mac?
> Vincent:  "Well, a Big Mac's a Big Mac, but they call it *Le Big-Mac.*"

McDonald's understood the value in having one proven way of flipping burgers, even if it goes by a different name. Royale with Cheese anyone? By using common policies and procedures, even with some cultural culinary tweaks—(how about some mayonnaise on those fries)—the McDonald's experience should be comparable if you get a Happy Meal at one in Paris, France or a franchise in Paris, Texas. McDonald's wanted to apply this same logic to whistleblowers, and how they should be treated similarly in both the United States and France. That is when the problem started. Employees could report anonymously in the United States, but the French looked at whistleblowers through a different lens, especially those trying to those trying to keep their identity private.

> Say whistle-blower in Germany, however, and the term most likely conjures up memories of the Gestapo, Adolf Hitler's secret police. In France, the term evokes images of the Vichy regime's collaboration with the Nazis and of neighbors ratting out one another.
>
> So it's probably no wonder that Germany and France have taken the lead in resisting provisions of Sarbanes-Oxley that shield from retaliation corporate whistle-blowers who report fraud and other financial irregularities. "Whistle-blowers are looked at as informants, particularly in France and Germany," says Boston employment and privacy lawyer Mark E. Schreiber. "That goes back to World War II."[24]

McDonald's was sandwiched between these two all-beef patties, trying to comply with U.S. and French regulators—(even if it held the "special sauce, lettuce, cheese, pickles, onions on a sesame seed bun"). In 2005, the fast-food chain wanted to implement a global whistleblower antiretaliation policy that satisfied Sarbanes-Oxley, but French regulators originally refused to allow protection for anonymous reporters.

> While such (whistleblower reporting) systems have raised few legal challenges in the United States, they have been under attack in Europe. Earlier this year the *Commission Nationale de l'Informatique et des Libertés* ("the CNIL") (the French independent administrative authority protecting privacy and personal data) initially ruled that such systems violated the French Data Protection Act of January 6, 1978, as amended on August 6, 2004 ("the Act"). This apparent conflict between the United States and French law resulted in anxious confusion and concern for many global organizations doing business in both countries.[25]

Would McDonald's need to carve out French employees from its worldwide helpline policies and procedures? This piecemeal approach would permit whistleblower protections for anonymous reports if they originated within the United States. The same company would have to tell its employees located in France that this type of complaint wasn't allowed. This could create an administrative nightmare. The CNIL took a bite of the problem by initiating talks between the U.S. and European authorities, along with trade unions, to seek a compromise. On November 10, 2005, the CNIL adopted guidelines to allow whistleblower protection, with some restraints, including:

- Limiting the scope of the whistleblower program;
- Restricting data collection to certain types of corporate misconduct;
- Controlling how the collected information is handled; and
- Making sure those accused by anonymous whistleblowers maintained their due process rights.[26]

With its global whistleblowing crisis averted, McDonald's could now focus on what knickknack to include in its next promotion and whether it should reoffer McRibs one more time.

### EU Whistleblowing Protection

Values-based leaders doing business in Europe should understand that continent's rules and regulations. Before 2019, whistleblowing laws across the EU were fragmented and inconsistent. Companies risked playing retaliation roulette in the European casino of commerce. What would happen if the wheel of misfortune spun, and the ball landed in a country that had effective whistleblower protection laws—like France or the United Kingdom? If an organization inappropriately disciplined a reporter there, the plaintiff might get a big payout in a lawsuit. Do the same thing in countries that didn't offer protection and the company would win.

To make the odds more even, EU countries agreed to a common Whistleblower Protection Directive—(the "Directive"). A December 17, 2021 deadline was set by the EU for each member country to transpose the Directive requirements into their own national laws. This Directive would protect the public interest by having minimum standards for all EU members. It defended those who spoke up in good faith about violations of EU laws.

> In practice, the Directive requires organisations in all EU member states with 250 or more employees to establish a well-defined reporting channel and procedures to allow people to report concerns regarding illegal activities. Smaller organisations of 50 or more people will have until 2023.[27]

These common procedures include:

- Reports could be verbal or in writing, and the company had to provide a secure process to receive them;
- Organizations had to acknowledge receipt of the complaint within seven days;
- Whistleblowers had to receive some feedback within three months of filing their concerns;
- Companies must designate an impartial person to handle the reports;
- Organizations must keep records of every report received while respecting the whistleblower's confidentiality.[28]

Each member country will develop its own laws regarding these questions. These patchwork policies could lead to confusion for companies operating across several borders. So, how should these multinational companies proceed?

> The more practical way to consider all of this is to put in place a process that meets the relative standard of the EU Directive as it currently stands. Use that same process on a worldwide basis as an overall strategy. If Denmark adopts a more rigorous standard, such as requiring acknowledgement of the report in five days instead of seven, then the company can evaluate if that is a best practice they want to adopt or instead that only under specific circumstances would they meet this higher standard.[29]

The Whistleblower Protection Directive included a broad definition of what would be considered retaliation including:

- Suspension;
- Demotion;
- Transfers;
- Withholding training;
- Bad performance reviews;
- Discipline;
- Reprimands or financial penalty;
- Harassment, discrimination;
- Failure to convert temporary employment into a permanent one;
- Failure to renew employment contract, reputational harm:
  o Including social media, blacklisting from the industry;
- Early termination;
- Cancelling license or permit;
- Psychiatric referral.[30]

This Directive also reversed the burden of proving retaliation by creating a presumption of reprisal if any of these job actions were imposed against the whistleblower. Organizations hoping to overcome this new presumption need a well-documented case about what nonretaliatory reasons it had to deal negatively with a whistleblower. Without this evidence, losing organizations face varying sanctions because the EU Whistleblower Directive mandated members shall institute proportionate penalties against companies that retaliated.

### Public Interest Disclosure Act 1998

Post-Brexit, the United Kingdom wasn't obligated to follow EU directives, including the Whistleblower Protection Directive. Fortunately for people reporting problems, the United Kingdom was considered to have strong whistleblower protection with its 1998 Public Interest Disclosure Act (PIDA). PIDA differed from the EU Whistleblower Protection Directive in several ways:

- PIDA addressed "workers," including employees, contractors, trainees, and agency staff. The Directive cast a wider net by also protecting "self-employed people, shareholders and board members (including non-executives), as well as 'facilitators' (these are individuals connected to the whistle-blower in a work-context, such as colleagues and relatives, and legal entities associated with the whistle-blower)."
- The Directive requires organizations with more than 50 employees—(after December of 2023)—to develop internal reporting channels to receive complaints. PIDA does not.
- The Directive mandates organizations acknowledge receipt of a report within seven days and provide feedback within three months of receipt. This is not the case with PIDA
- Under the Directive, whistleblowers who establish some disciplinary action was taken against them, shift the burden of proof to the organization to show it was justified. With PIDA, the burden remains with the plaintiff.

Even if the United Kingdom isn't required to adopt the EU Whistleblower Directive, it could make sense to follow some of its guidelines to promote cross-border consistency.

The False Claims Act, Sarbanes-Oxley, Dodd-Frank, PIDA, and the EU Whistleblower Directive are laws that offer some form of whistleblower protection or incentives. Given this, what internal algorithm does a whistleblower use to calculate whether to report and to whom?

## Case Study 4.3—Roger Boisjoly and the Space Shuttle Challenger Disaster

Roger Boisjoly was a senior scientist at Morton Thiokol and, in 1986, worked on the Space Shuttle Challenger project. He studied the company's O-rings, which were used to stop flammable fuel from escaping the booster rockets. These rings were designed for launches when the temperature was greater than 53° Fahrenheit, and the engineers told NASA that cold weather would cause the O-rings to stiffen and not function properly. On the morning of the launch—January 28, 1986—there were icicles on the Challenge due to the freezing weather. Boisjoly warned Thiokol and NASA about the inherent dangers of launching under these conditions but was overruled. Tragically, the Challenger suffered a "major malfunction" and exploded 73 seconds after liftoff.

In the aftermath of the disaster, former Secretary of State—William Rogers—chaired the "Roger's Commission." It was established to determine the cause of the accident, and Roger Boisjoly was called to appear. Boisjoly had to decide how he would respond to questions:

> And I also learned subsequently that there are only three decision-making choices—exit, voice, and loyalty—and that I had exercised voice my whole career. When I had seen others capitulate, they were exercising loyalty. And when I saw people in meetings remain silent, even though they had just as much talent as I had, I understood that they were exercising the exit option.[31]

Boisjoly refused to keep his mouth shut like others who exited the problem. He was honor-bound to honesty—not blind loyalty to Thiokol. He chose to give voice to the facts and speak truth to power for those seven dead astronauts who could no longer talk for themselves.

Roger Boisjoly made the tough call to tell the world what caused the explosion on January 28, 1986. What process did he, and other whistleblowers, use to decide whether to "raise their hand" and come forward?

## Inside the Mind of the Whistleblower

### Awareness

Whistleblowers can only report on things they know about, so the first step is discovering potential problems. Since 2000, the Ethics and Compliance Initiative—(ECI)—has conducted bi-annual longitudinal surveys analyzing problems at the workplace. ECI surveys from 2000 to 2020 measured what percent of employees observed misconduct. This ranged from a high of 54 percent in 2007 to a low of 45 percent in 2011, so in any given year, around half of the employees surveyed saw something they thought was wrong.

In addition to seeing problems, employees need to understand the reporting process. Having a hotline can be an important alternative to speaking directly with your boss, especially if that person may be involved in the dilemma. Unfortunately, a 2017 Fraud Survey by Ernst & Young found that four out of five employees didn't know their companies even had a hotline. Values-based leaders need an effective communication strategy to get the word out about the existence and the proper way to use the helpline.

### Retaliation

One reason employees may be unwilling to blow the whistle is they fear retaliation. This type of managerial revenge isn't always direct. While some whistleblowers may be fired immediately after reporting a problem, others might suffer a loss of status or friendships inside the company. Maybe they were in line for a promotion, but after disclosing their concerns, the job went to someone less qualified. Perhaps their entire team used to go out for drinks every Friday after work. Now, the rest of the team still goes out, but the whistleblower is no longer welcome.

They may even find themselves banished to the corporate version of Siberia. This is what happened to Walter Tamosaitis, a former contract worker at an Energy Department installation in Washington state. He reported that radioactive waste was being improperly processed and was immediately transferred to a windowless office in the basement.

> "It was so lonely," he said. One day, there was a big snowstorm outside. In the basement, the phone rang. It was his wife, who'd seen a TV report that his workplace had been shut down. He went upstairs: lights out. Doors locked. Nobody told him.
>
> "I thought the Rapture had occurred," Tamosaitis said. "And I said, 'Well, [expletive]. I'm the good guy, it can't be the Rapture. *I* should be gone, and they should be here.'"[32]

These knee-jerk punishments seem petty and miss the mark that a values-based leader like President Lincoln understood. He refused to operate in an "echo chamber," only being around people who agreed with him. As his biographer Doris Kearns Goodwin wrote—"Good leadership requires you to surround yourself with people of diverse perspectives who can disagree with you without fear of retaliation."

### Agency

Once someone knows about a potential problem, will they report it or remain quiet? This might depend on how they interpret a quote attributed to a values-based leader—Dr. Martin Luther King, Jr.—"In the end we will remember not the words of our enemies, but the silence of our friends." The response may change by how two anagrams of the word "s-i-l-e-n-t" are arranged. Can they "e-n-l-i-s-t" someone they trust, who will "l-i-s-t-e-n"? While some only pay attention to the squeaky wheel, former BP CEO— Bob Dudley—as a principled principal understood the importance of "listening to the quietest voice in the room." All wheels, not just the squeaky ones, need grease and proper care.

Leaders must be willing to listen to problems. But that isn't enough. Actions speak louder than words, so how will VBLs respond to these complaints? Another values-based leader—Winston Churchill—said, "I never worry about action but only inaction." Whistleblowers share Churchill's fear. Why should they risk their jobs, careers, and even family, if their company won't act on their concerns?

There is a difference between managerial inaction and a manager's inability to share the results of an investigation with the whistleblower. To protect the accused employee's privacy rights, a values-based leader may choose not to disclose any disciplinary action taken against the accused. The target may have been privately disciplined, lost salary, bonuses, promotion opportunities, and on the verge of being pushed out of the company. Unfortunately, if the whistleblower still sees the subject of their complaint showing up to work every day, the whistleblower may think their complaints were ignored.

This is where trust comes into play. Does the VBL promote a culture in which whistleblowers can express their concerns, actions may be taken but not readily apparent, and the whistleblowers still believe they were taken seriously? Do employees still have faith in their leaders? VBLs need to carefully nurture this virtue, but it will be compromised if they attempt to find out who anonymously reported a problem. In 2016, Jes Staley—then the CEO of Barclays—became the poster child of this type of "trust buster" when he tried to unmask a whistleblower who anonymously filed a complaint with Barclays' board against one of Staley's friends. While human nature, friendship, and even ego may have played a role in Staley's actions, he paid a partial price for his "mistake."

> UK financial regulators announced Friday that Staley had been fined £642,430 ($870,000) after he "failed to act with due skill, care and diligence." In addition, Barclays said it would claw back £500,000 ($680,000) of Staley's 2016 pay over the incident.... In addition to the fine, Barclays (BCS) will be required to report each year on how it handles whistleblowing, the regulators said. The American banking executive admitted last year that he had "made a mistake" by attempting to find out who authored an anonymous letter that raised concerns about a senior Barclays employee.[33]

Barclays also suffered by losing its employees' trust. Whistleblowing cases dropped by almost a third in the year following Staley's fine.

## Case Study 4.4—Michael Woodford and Olympus

The *Urban Dictionary* defines citizens of Liverpool, England as "scousers" who are "generally welcoming, fun loving, hardworking and a talented breed of people." Paul McCartney is a scouser, and so is Michael Woodford—the former CEO of Olympus. Woodford worked in a British subsidiary of Olympus—KeyMed—for much of his career and went on to run businesses for the Japanese multinational in the United States and Europe. After 30 years as a "salaryman," he was tapped to be the first *gaijin*—(non-Japanese)— president of the parent company—Olympus Corporation. His greatest supporter was the chair and company CEO, Tsuyoshi Kikukawa. Kikukawa saw Woodford as a no-nonsense Western businessperson who could help with cost-cutting and other challenging strategies Japanese leaders were reluctant to enact.

Michael Woodford's company turnaround was going as planned until he discovered a distressing story regarding Olympus from a little-known Japanese business magazine—Facta. The article detailed how Olympus wrote off approximately $1.7 billion in company debt by acquiring three "Mickey Mouse" organizations in 2008. One company sold face cream. A second made microwave dishes, and the third was a recycling business. In addition to this, Olympus paid a $687 million consulting fee to acquire another company—Gyrus. The typical fee for this type of recommendation was approximately one percent of the two billion dollar purchase. That would equate to $20,000,000, paid only after thousands of hours of due diligence and numerous binders of data compiled by the consultant were delivered to the client. Instead, Olympus agreed to an amount equaling 36 percent of the purchase price for a one-page memo by the consultant. Nice work if you can get it.

As a values-based leader, Michael Woodford felt compelled to dig deeper and immediately scheduled a lunch meeting to discuss his concerns with Kikukawa. The meal showcased a stunning array of sumptuous sushi at the head table. Instead of his favorite raw fish, Mr. Woodford's plate featured a "manky tuna sandwich." The message was clear—"Be quiet, and don't stick your nose into this business." As a VBL, Michael Woodford didn't heed this threat and hired PwC to investigate, which confirmed his worst fears.

After another damning feature in Facta—this time allegedly link-ing Olympus' fraud with "anti-social forces"—(read: the Japanese crime syndicate known as the Yakuza)—Mr. Woodford feared for his personal safety. Undeterred, Woodford sent letters to Olympus' board, its non-executives, and the senior partners of E&Y around the world, calling for Kikukawa's resignation. The next board meeting was supposedly scheduled to address the topic, but instead, upon entering the board-room, Kikukawa called for a snap vote to fire Mr. Woodford. The board seemed eager to please Kikukawa and terminated their *gaijin* president on the spot.

Michael Woodford attempted to launch a proxy battle to gain con-trol of Olympus but was unsuccessful, with Japanese institutional share-holders unwilling to stand by him. He returned to the United Kingdom to be with his family. Unfortunately, his former Olympus friends weren't supportive.

> Once I had been ousted from Olympus, my relationship with many
> of those left on the inside became strained. Former close colleagues
> whom I'd known for years suddenly treated me like some sort of
> leper and studiously avoided all contact with me. There seemed to
> be an insidious pressure on some to have nothing to do with me.
> I had been deemed a contaminant. I was suddenly *persona non
> grata* and couldn't understand just what I had done wrong.[34]

As a proud "scouser," Woodford's favorite football—(soccer)—club was Liverpool FC, nicknamed "The Reds." The Reds club's theme song played before each game was a rousing rendition of Roger and Ham-merstein's "You'll Never Walk Alone" from the musical Carousel. The irony is that Michael Woodford, along with many other whistleblowers, "would always walk alone."

## Conclusion

How whistleblowers are perceived might depend on which party walks into an attorney's office. In 2004, Victor Schachter—an employment partner at Fenwick & West—representing organizations, stated, "I've seen a mini explosion of whistle-blower claims by people who are marginal performers, if not malingerers." Jeffrey Ross—an attorney representing whistleblowers—had a different point of view. "[O]nce high-performing, well respected employees blow the whistle, suddenly they become, in retrospect, terrible, if not incompetent employees." Why is there so much *"sturm und drang"* about this in the workplace? Principled principles should encourage reporting potential violations, raised in good faith, as soon as possible. Learning about these incidents early on can help VBLs tamp down these smoldering sparks before they become raging infernos.

> I've found many examples of people at all levels who created positive change without ruining their careers.... I call [these] people ... *competently courageous* because they create the right conditions for action by establishing a strong internal reputa- tion and by improving their fallback options in case things go poorly; they carefully choose their battles, discerning whether a given opportunity to act makes sense in light of their values, the timing, and their broader objectives; they maximize the odds of in-the-moment success by managing the messaging and emotions; and they follow up to preserve relationships and marshal commitment.[35]

Values-based leaders should create a culture in which people like Haugen, Rowley, Watkins, Cooper, Boisjoly, Tamosaitis, Woodford, and others can be role models for competently courageous behavior. These men and women can act in the public interest while still being considered loyal to their organizations.

# What Happens if a Leader's Company Gets in Trouble?

Values-based leaders need to understand how to prevent violations. Those that can't be prevented, need to be detected and dealt with as soon as possible. This chapter investigates how organizations can find and fix their problems and the fines for failing to address them. Regarding violations, it will explore fraud in general and the Foreign Corrupt Practices Act (FCPA) in particular. Remediation will be addressed by the 1991 Federal Sentencing Guidelines for Organizations (FSGO). These were initiated to encourage VBLs to develop effective ethics and compliance programs. They incentivize self-reporting to the government and cooperation with any subsequent investigations. The FSGO proposed seven minimum elements of an effective ethics and compliance program. The question VBLs need to ask is whether their organizations have:

- Policies and procedures to address concerns;
- High-level oversight with someone like a Chief Compliance Officer;
- Due diligence in the hiring process;
- Effective training, including its board;
- Monitoring and internal controls;
- Consistent enforcement throughout the company; and
- Continuous improvement.

Risk assessment wasn't a separate element of the FSGO but was considered an overarching theme running throughout the design and implementation of the program. This chapter compares a company that did almost everything right—(Goodco)—with one that is the poster child for all things wrong regarding corporate misconduct—(Badco). The Department of Justice—(DoJ)—and federal judges will give significantly better treatment to companies that had an effective ethics and compliance program, cooperated with the government investigation and accepted responsibility afterwards, compared to those that had high-level officials involved with the violation and a pervasive tolerance of the illegal activity by the organization.

For years, ethics and compliance professionals were unsure whether their programs would receive credit from the Department of Justice. In 2023, the government developed a series of questions values-based leaders could answer to determine if their organization qualifies for favorable treatment. The DoJ wants proof that the company's programs are:

- Well designed;
- Adequately resourced to function effectively; and
- Working in practice.

The answers to these questions determine what action the Department of Justice would take once it began investigating corporate wrongdoing. Its prosecutorial options are:

- Seek disgorgement of ill-gotten gains;
- Decline to prosecute the company;
- Agree to a Nonprosecution Agreement—(NPA);
- Pursue a Deferred Prosecution Agreement—(DPA).

If the defendant corporation doesn't meet the requirements for these options, the DoJ could always take the case to trial. Criminal fines and sanctions were typically far greater when this occurred.

Marketing and Ethics researchers are also exploring the "value of values," and initial studies show consumers are willing to pay more money for products sold by companies with effective compliance programs.

# #5—The Science of Compliance

## Introduction

Edward, First Baron Thurlow posed the question—"Did you expect a corporation to have a conscience, when it has no soul to be damned, and no body to be kicked?" He was making a metaphysical observation about organizations, but he forgot to mention that first they could be forced to pay back their ill-gotten gains. In addition, they could be fined and even debarred—(stopped) from doing business with the government in the future. One more possible penalty imposed could be having an outside monitor appointed to oversee their activities.

So, what is the corporate calculus of risk, and how might executives determine the price of vice? Here are the variables for plotting the graph of graft:

What is the likelihood of detection  $\rightarrow$  = A

Multiply this by the probable fine   $\rightarrow$  = B.

$$A*B \rightarrow = C, \text{ the cost of the crime.}$$

If the expected outcome was greater than the criminal sanction, the "rational" wrongdoer might think—"why not sin away?" This calculation could have been common before Chapter 8 of FSGO was enacted by the U.S. Sentencing Commission—(the USSC)—in 1991. These organizational guidelines established a sentencing rubric that would reward certain values-based behaviors with fine reductions and punish others with fine multipliers. This carrot-and-stick approach to sentencing noncorporeal, soulless entities helped create an entire compliance and ethics industry. Law firms and consultants now offer surveys, monitoring, evaluations, and training for companies on areas ranging from corporate culture to whistleblower hotlines and everything in between. Are you interested in Enterprise Risk Management dashboards, helplines and staffing, data analytics, ethics workshops or advice about Diversity Equity and Inclusion, Anti-money laundering, Know Your Customer, Antitrust or the False Claims Act? There are a host of providers happy to accommodate—for a hefty fee.

## The Foreign Corrupt Practices Act—(FCPA)

Principled principals need to be aware of risk areas within their businesses and then develop strategies to minimize them. Most of this chapter applies to all federal laws that a business might break. This section focuses on FCPA violations as examples of how the DoJ and federal courts treat offending organizations. In 1977, the U.S. House of Representatives discussed its rationale for adopting the FCPA.

> The payment of bribes to influence the acts or decisions of foreign officials, foreign political parties or candidates for foreign political office is unethical…. But not only is it unethical, it is bad business as well…. In short, it rewards corruption instead of efficiency and puts pressure on ethical enterprises to lower their standards or risk losing business. Bribery of foreign officials by some American companies casts a shadow on all U.S. companies.

The FCPA was passed during a post-Watergate anticorruption era in Washington. Just like Kevin Costner's "Field of Dreams," the American hope was that "if we build it—(anti-bribery legislation)—they—(other countries)—will come." Unfortunately for U.S. values-based leaders, the rest of the world didn't "follow the leader" until the Organization for Economic Cooperation and Development—(OECD)—criminalized these bribes in 1999. The old joke before the OECD enacted this convention was—"A U.S. businessperson who bribes a foreign official could end up in jail, and their company might pay a large fine. A German company might get a generous tax deduction!" How "unlevel" was that playing field? At the turn of the last century, OECD signatory countries agreed it should be a crime to bribe foreign officials, and companies shouldn't receive tax write-offs for these illegal payments.

## U.S. Sentencing Commission and the Principles of Federal Prosecution of Organizations

What factors does the USSC use to determine whether the direction and magnitude of the fines should go up or down? Charges could be reduced for organizations that followed the "3 C's":

- Compliance;
- Cooperation; and
- Contrition.

Values-based companies can receive a significant fine reduction by establishing an effective ethics and compliance program, helping with government investigations, accepting responsibility, and agreeing not to be repeat offenders. Other organizations could pay several times their base fines, based on a combination of considerations:

- The number of employees;
- Whether a high-level person within the organization condoned the activity; or
- Whether organizational tolerance of the illegal activity was pervasive.

## Case Study 5.1—*Compliance v. Defiance*

Let's put the U.S. Sentencing Guidelines along with the DoJ's Evaluation of Corporate Compliance Programs to the test and compare the economic impact on two hypothetical companies—"Goodco" and "Badco." Both companies have more than 5,000 employees with at least one staff member being caught giving multiple bribes to foreign officials, totaling $1,000,000 apiece. Both acts violate the FCPA, but that is where the similarity ends.

### Badco

The CEO of Badco's only value echoed Enron's informal motto—"Get Rich or Get Fired!" That CEO shared the same sentiment about rule-following with Wirecard CEO—Markus Braun—when he stated—"Compliance is crap."[1] Badco's lead salesperson—Really Rotten Ralph—was known to cut ethical corners to close big deals and receive large commissions. Their compliance program and internal controls modulated somewhere between lax and nonexistent. Really Rotten Ralph used a third-party agent who was the brother of the Minister of Defense in the target country. That agent demanded Badco pay them a fee twice the going rate of comparable third parties. That money was to be deposited into the agent's offshore bank account in the Cayman Islands—(preferably in nonsequential, unmarked U.S. $20 bills). The agent then paid the bribe to his brother with the excess commission to close the deal. Badco's Chief Marketing Officer knew about the scheme and approved Really Rotten Ralph's tactics to complete the transaction. These bribes were reported internally to senior management, who ignored the complaints because they all got large bonuses based on the misconduct. A whistleblower finally informed the DoJ about the violation, and they are now conducting an extensive investigation into Badco. Even after being notified about the government's scrutiny, Badco refused to fire Really Rotten Ralph and paid for his high-priced outside legal counsel to fight the claim. The company also rejected the government's request to cooperate with the investigation and wouldn't apologize for their (mis)behavior.

### Goodco

Goodco took a very different approach. The CEO was a values-based leader and was proud of the company's compliance and ethics programs. It also had a very sophisticated system of internal controls. Goodco was ranked by Ethisphere as one of "The World's Most Ethical Companies" for 10 years in a row. Their principled principals reinforced the culture of compliance with both words and deeds, and Goodco conducted investigations that were both quick and thorough whenever potential violations surfaced. During a random audit, it discovered the sophisticated bribery scheme by a lower-level salesperson—Subtly Rotten Ralph. As soon as it started its internal probe, Goodco's VBLs alerted the DoJ about the potential problem, asking for time to complete the review. After the investigation, Goodco's values-based leaders delivered all the relevant information and documents to the DoJ (translated into English at Goodco's expense), cooperated with the government in Subtly Rotten Ralph's criminal prosecution, and fired him on the spot. The company's VBLs investigated Subtly Rotten Ralph's supervisors and concluded the managers didn't know, nor should they reasonably have been expected to know, about his misconduct. Goodco's principled principals accepted responsibility, cooperated with the investigation, and made appropriate corrections to its already world-class compliance and ethics program, along with minor tweaks to its internal controls.

### Fines at Goodco v. Badco

Even though both companies engaged in $1,000,000 worth of bribes, would Goodco and Badco be treated differently by the DoJ? Yes, very differently. Badco's leaders are the poster children for every reason the government wants to prosecute organizations. They were a bunch of belligerent, obstructionist, arrogant, nose-thumbing rule-breakers. Goodco's values-based leaders were the polar opposite and did almost everything right—(except prevent these bribes). Based on the multiple illegal payments to a foreign official, totaling $1,000,000, according to the Federal Sentencing Guidelines Manual, Goodco and Badco both start the penalty party with a potential $30,000,000 base fine. The amounts vary significantly after that. (For an in-depth analysis of how these fines are calculated, please see Appendix I.)

The fact that Badco had more than 5,000 employees and high-level personnel—(Really Rotten Ralph)—participated in the bribery could multiply the $30,000,000 by a factor of 4 for a potential $120,000,000 fine. Goodco's world-class compliance and ethics program, substantial cooperation and acceptance of responsibility could reduce the fine by 95 percent, for a potential $1,500,000 penalty. To paraphrase Billy Mays—(Oxiclean), Vince—(Shamwow), or the original late-night infomercial spokesperson Ron Popeil—(Chop-O-Matic)—"but wait—there's more." Because of Goodco's model behavior and self-disclosure in this FCPA violation, the DoJ has an added "sweetener" of reducing the potential fine by up to 75 percent off the low end of the U.S. Sentencing Guidelines range. Given this, Goodco's fine could be whittled down further to $375,000 (25 percent of $1,500,000). A four times multiplier versus a 98.75 percent reduction is the equivalent of a 320:1 fine differential, depending on how a company reacts to violations. This "ethics curve" helps make the case for leading with values.

## The (Magnificent) Seven Requirements for an Effective Ethics and Compliance Program

Seven shows up repeatedly in both nature and entertainment. It is the number of:

- Seas;
- Wonders of the world;
- Notes on a musical scale;
- Days in the week;
- Continents; and
- Colors in a rainbow.

Cinematically it is how many:

- Dwarves who befriend Snow White;
- Years of marriage it takes before developing an "itch";
- Samurais needed to defend a Japanese village; and
- Kingdoms in Westeros.

While rolling a "Lucky 7" with dice might make you money at a craps table, it is also the number of FSGO "minimum requirements" for an effective ethics and compliance program. These elements focus on:

- Policies and procedures;
- People in charge of compliance and ethics functions;
- Due diligence in the hiring process;
- Training;
- Monitoring and auditing;
- Consistency; and
- Corrective actions.

Since its inception in 1991, values-based leaders have tried to figure out what is the best way to implement these organizational guidelines to satisfy the DoJ and federal judges. The DoJ put some meat on these seven bare bones with a series of evaluations of Corporate Compliance

Programs in 2017, 2019, 2020, and 2023. The 212 government inter-rogatories exceeded the number of questions over four nights of Jeopardy. The answers will determine if the company should be:

- Prosecuted;
- Subject to criminal fines and penalties; and
- Sanctioned by imposing a corporate monitor.

These extensive queries were offshoots of three fundamental ones:

1. Was the compliance program well designed?
2. Was it applied earnestly and in good faith, and does it have adequate resources to function effectively?
3. Does it work in practice?

The DoJ didn't want companies to apply a cookie-cutter template in which "one size compliance program fits all." Instead of buying a pre-packaged "insert company name here" Microsoft Word file, values-based leaders should shepherd their organizations through a thoughtful and deliberative process to determine what compliance and ethics program works best for them. The DoJ also considers the company's size, indus-try, geographic footprint, and regulatory landscape in determining what actions it should pursue.

## Was the Program Well Designed?

Values-based leaders will have "3 swings" before "striking out" in the argument that its compliance program was effective. The DoJ will eval-uate the company's program at the time of the violation. If its program is weak or nonexistent—strike one. The next hack happens at the time of the charging decision. Again— if it was still ineffective—strike two. The final plate appearance occurs at the time of the resolution of the violation. If VBLs made significant improvements to develop an effec-tive compliance program, it could wallop a home run toward limit-ing its penalty. If not—three whiffs and it is out of luck in hoping for favorable treatment.

Prosecutors will review how the company:

- Conducted its risk assessments;
- Developed its policies and procedures;
- Managed its training and communication;
- Implemented its confidential reporting mechanism and investigation process;
- Reviewed how third parties are dealt with, and whether it exercised due diligence regarding mergers and acquisitions.

Did the principled principals' messaging, training, and incentive structure clearly state that misconduct was unacceptable? Was there undue pressure placed on employees to break laws and regulations?

### Risk Assessment

Risk assessment was not included in the original FSGO when it was enacted in 1991. Instead of becoming the "8th minimum requirement," it appeared in the 2004 U.S. Sentencing Guidelines Amendments as an "overarching" element of an effective program. One risk values-based leaders face deals with hiring. FSGO §8B2.1(b)(3) recognized this by stating,

> The organization shall use reasonable efforts not to include within the substantial authority personnel of the organization any individual whom the organization knew or should have known through the exercise of due diligence, has engaged in illegal activities or other conduct inconsistent with an effective compliance and ethics program.

VBLs should do everything possible to investigate how prospective employees acted at their previous workplaces. Were they convicted of bribery, involved in embezzlement schemes, or accused of harassing co-workers? This information could provide important insight into how the employee might behave at a new company.

While principled principals are expected to do background checks, it may be difficult to find former employers willing to do more than verify dates of employment or the ex-employee's job title. Previous employers fear defamation lawsuits and are typically under no affirmative duty to "spill the tea" on their ex-employees. Even with this understanding of the low probability of getting useful data, values-based leaders interviewing prospective employees should use their best efforts to obtain this information in a legal and ethical fashion. Well-documented efforts may become a defense in a subsequent "negligent hiring" lawsuit brought by victims of similar misconduct.

### Policies and Procedures

What kind of paperwork do VBLs maintain that shows they promote good behavior and punish violations? FSGO §8B2.1(b)(1) states, "An organization shall develop standards and procedures to help detect and prevent criminal conduct." Almost all companies, both large and small, used to have thick binders bursting with policies. They resembled textbooks for some unmotivated students—rarely opened and collecting dust in the corner. Companies still have policies and procedures, but the plastic portfolios have been replaced by flash drives or links on their corporate intranet sites.

### Training and Communication

FSGO §8B2.1.(4)(A) focuses on the training component of an Effective Ethics and Compliance Program:

> The organization shall take reasonable steps to communicate periodically and in a practical manner its standards and procedures, and other aspects of the compliance and ethics program, to the individuals ... (members of the governing authority, high-level personnel, employees and the company's agents) by conducting effective training programs and otherwise disseminating information appropriate to such individuals' respective roles and responsibilities.

Once policies and procedures have been developed, values-based leaders need to deliver the message through effective training at all levels, including the board of directors.

The DoJ recognized that training shouldn't be "one size fits all" regarding length and the target audience. Shorter "microlearning" sessions, tailored toward a specific risk to a limited audience, may be more effective than longer generic training directed to all employees. A product safety engineer only doing business in the United States may not need to know the nuances of the FCPA. In-depth training about this law could be much more relevant for an international salesperson doing business in a country that Transparency International rates as being perceived as highly corrupt. Communicating and reinforcing a company's antibribery policy to that second staffer could help minimize corporate and individual fines, along with reducing or eliminating possible jail time.

Effective training encourages interaction and can be another way values-based leaders can gather information about potential problems. VBLs who create a trusting environment may encourage participants to come up during a workshop break, or after a session, and alert them about areas of concern. This might not happen during a "talking head" lecture, where the trainer read verbatim—(in a low, quiet, monotonous whisper)—the PowerPoint slide deck packed with as many legalistic Latin terms crammed into every square inch of the screen or monitor. Does the training seem to be more lecturing and scolding rather than inspiring and empowering? Is it a laundry list of "thou shalt nots" written by lawyers for lawyers? Values-based leaders should evaluate employee comprehension and effectiveness of the training, not use it in anticipation as a potential trial exhibit. Does the company throw associates "under the bus" by arguing that the misconduct was all the employee's fault because the action was specifically prohibited on bullet #18 in slide #146 in the mandatory annual compliance training every employee received—(even if the font was so small you needed to squint while using a magnifying glass to read it)?

### Confidential Reporting and Subsequent Investigations

The DoJ is very interested in how principled principals deal with whistleblowing. Are employees aware of their company helpline or hotline, and are they allowed to report confidentially or anonymously? Can employees report problems without fear of retaliation? Are company investigations conducted objectively and independently, and are they well documented?

(For more information about Confidential Reporting and Subsequent Investigations, please review Lesson #4—"What to Do When Someone Finds Problems at Work?")

### Third-Party Management

Outside agents are often used in doing deals in foreign countries because they speak the language, understand the local culture and customs, and may have preestablished relationships with decision makers. Before the FCPA was passed in 1977, U.S. businesses tried to distance themselves from an agent's illegal actions by arguing, "it was the third-party paying the bribe. Not us." This "see no evil, hear no evil, speak no evil" attitude was specifically countered when the FCPA was enacted. Organizations are now responsible for their agent's behavior, along with its officers, directors, or employees who offered bribes to foreign officials to obtain or retain business.

Values-based leaders can no longer outsource responsibility and criminal liability. They must investigate and ask questions, especially when a third party is charging fees significantly higher than comparable agents in that region. The intermediary may argue that their higher commission is justified because they are more effective in closing deals. That answer isn't good enough for the government. VBLs should use due diligence and dig deeper. One tool of the trade that might make the "digging" easier is for the values-based leader to retain the right to audit the third party's books. This could help determine whether the excess fees were used to bribe foreign officials. Another "red flag" is when fees inexplicably change from month to month. VBLs should use their best efforts to negotiate fixed fees for third parties.

### Mergers and Acquisitions

It's common for acquiring companies to conduct preacquisition financial and legal due diligence on potential targets. That's because the acquirer not only buys the assets of the acquired one but also inherits

its liabilities. There are numerous litigation concerns if the acquired company was involved in illegal activity, like bribery. Without adequate oversight, misconduct by the acquired company may continue even after it is integrated into the acquiring company.

The DoJ doesn't want to prohibit mergers and acquisitions, especially if the acquiring company can make the acquired company more compliant. On September 15, 2022, Deputy Attorney General Lisa Monaco memorialized this sentiment in a speech to New York University when she said:

> Separately, we do not want to discourage acquisitions that result in reformed and improved compliance structures. We will not treat as recidivists companies with a proven track record of compliance that acquire companies with a history of compliance problems, so long as those problems are promptly and properly addressed post-acquisition.[2]

Once the acquisition is complete, values-based leaders should use their best efforts to incorporate the target into their own compliance program and internal controls.

All these factors—risk assessment, policies and procedures, training and communication, confidential reporting, third-party management, and mergers and acquisitions—are parts of a well-designed compliance and ethics program. The next question focuses on whether principled principals "put their money where their mouths are?"

## Is It Adequately Resourced and Empowered to Function Effectively?

Prosecutors should evaluate whether the VBL's initiatives were part of a "paper program" or one implemented in an effective manner.

### Corporate Commitment to Compliance

The DoJ will enquire whether mid- and senior-level managers "buy into" the VBL's commitment to a culture of compliance, or have they pressured subordinates to engage in misconduct? Have values-based leaders communicated their commitment to ethics and compliance, and do they model good ethical behavior?

(For more information on managers as role models, please see the section titled—"Tone of the Organization" as part of Lesson #1, "How Do Things Get Done Around Here?")

### Autonomy and Resources

Do VBLs have anyone overseeing compliance and ethics issues? Both the DoJ and the USSC recognize that this can depend on the size of the enterprise. Smaller companies probably can't afford a person or group dedicated solely to ethics and compliance. This doesn't mean small companies can ignore following the rules. One employee may need to perform multiple roles, including overseeing compliance issues. If the company is large enough to justify a stand-alone Chief Ethics and Compliance Officer—(CECO)—to whom do they report? The Board? Audit Committee? CEO? CFO? Internal Audit? Security? General Counsel—(GC)?

Does the CECO have a "seat at the table" during important meetings? If so, the follow-up question might be "which seat" and "which table?" Is the CECO off in the corner, just like being at the "kiddie table" during a Thanksgiving dinner, or are they prominently placed at something akin to King Arthur's "Round Table," next to the "big people" decision makers? CECOs should strive for more than settling to "be in the room where it happens." They need a "voice at the table." When other leaders are asking about the financial and legal considerations of a decision or transaction, is the CECO's opinion given comparable weight when raising the compliance, ethical, and corporate culture implications of these decisions?

FSGO §8B2.1.(2)(A) expects the Board of Directors to be knowledgeable about the compliance and ethics programs, so they can make informed decisions overseeing these initiatives. The Board needs to be aware of the potential problems through effective training. This can create some tension within organizations about how much access a Chief Ethics and Compliance Officer has to the Board. If they meet with the Board, will they have enough time to train them, as opposed to just reporting?

Reporting might mean a CECO gets less than an hour of the annual Board meeting and is only allowed to describe items like:

- The number of hotline calls received.
- How they plan on rolling out a new policy about gifts.
- The average time to close an investigation.

This can be important information but isn't necessarily training. Reporting can be passive and may not involve much interaction or engagement. Training is more dynamic, creating a dialogue between the CECO and the board members and raising awareness about the pressing ethical issues confronting the company.

## Incentives and Discipline

Does the values-based leader offer incentives for good behavior consistent with its compliance program? This could come in the form of certificates, stock options, receiving public recognition through a prestigious "President's Award," or something as small as a "Jiminy Cricket" plastic figurine when someone is observed acting ethically, advancing the company's values. Some companies include ethics as part of their bonuses, but the bar may be set very low and might not make up a significant portion of the award. This sends the message that ethics and compliance aren't that important. Dan Roach is a values-based leader and former Chief Compliance Officer at Dignity Health. He took a different approach toward executive compensation. To even qualify to "dip their toe" into the bonus pool, executives had to first meet the ethics metrics. In a 2013 *Wall Street Journal* article, Roach wrote:

> [A]t some companies, performance against compliance objectives gets weighed in bonus discussions. Not at Dignity. There, no hospital chief executive can even hope to talk about a bonus without clearing the bar on compliance objectives—so compliance is the *sine qua non* of executive compensation.[3]

Incentives can act as "the carrot," but the DoJ also recognizes the importance of discipline—"the stick." Principled principals may want to publicize sanitized case studies, demonstrating how they consistently punish violators of policies, procedures, laws, and regulations. Does the VBL send a clear message to all employees that unethical behavior won't be tolerated, regardless of the violator's position within the organization?

On March 3, 2023, Assistant Attorney General Kenneth Polite, Jr. announced a pilot program to encourage companies to "claw back" compensation from employees who broke laws to get their bonuses. He stated:

> If the company meets these factors and—in good faith—has initiated the process to recover such compensation at the time of resolution, our prosecutors will accord an additional fine reduction equal to the amount of any compensation that is recouped within the resolution term.

The DoJ understands that high-level executives might aggressively fight this clawback attempt, but it will still award a fine reduction of up to 25 percent of the amount the VBL attempted to recoup.

If the system of rewards and punishments is fairly administered and clearly communicated, employees are more likely to believe their values-based leaders are committed to compliance and ethics.

## Does It Work in Practice?

Ronald Regan is credited with describing an economist as someone who observes something happening, then thinks, "I wonder if it would work in theory?" While there may be plenty of economics professionals working at the DoJ, prosecutors don't necessarily focus on the theoretical aspect of that equation. They are more concerned about whether a compliance program actually works.

A cynic might argue that the only reason a company is being investigated by the DoJ is because it had a violation. Given that, by definition, the compliance program or system of internal controls must have failed. That would be a short-sighted dismissal of what could be a very effective program. This was demonstrated by our previous description of "Goodco." Perhaps their program didn't prevent the misconduct, but it was detected early on, and their VBLs immediately reported the problem to the government. Principled principals might have followed up with remediation efforts to prevent future violations. That is not a program that ought to be punished—it should be a role model. Both the DoJ and the USSC realized that perfection was not the standard. Good faith and due diligence should be. Both organizations memorialized Voltaire's quote, "The perfect should not be the enemy of the good."

The DoJ will explore:

- Whether VBLs assess the effectiveness of their compliance programs.
- Is there a process for:
  - Continuous improvement,
  - Testing,
  - Review,
  - Investigation, and
  - Analysis of remediation efforts?
- Have the values-based leaders conducted a "gap analysis" between their company's current state and an ideal one to determine its vulnerabilities? If so, do they have a plan to "plug the holes" in their program?
- Do VBLs conduct a "root cause analysis" of why violations occurred and make changes due to these "lessons learned" to prevent and detect similar misconduct in the future?

One example of root cause analysis involves going to the car on a cold winter morning, and it wouldn't start. This is where the "Five Whys" come into play.

- Observation—the car won't start.
  - Why?
- The battery is dead.
  - Why?
- The alternator isn't working.
  - Why?
- The belt is broken.
  - Why?

- It wasn't replaced in a timely fashion.
  - Why?
- *Root cause analysis—the maintenance manual was never read.*
  - What corrective action should be taken?
- Read the manual and follow the parts replacement schedule.

Have the values-based leaders made improvements to their company's compliance programs and internal controls? Have the VBLs engaged in meaningful testing while reviewing their policies, procedures, and internal controls? These types of questions were posed when Total Quality Management guru—W. Edwards Deming—developed the PDCA —(Plan, Do, Check, Act)—cycle. Risk assessment is also an important part of the planning phase. Once analyzed, principled principals should develop policies and procedures to mitigate these risks.

The answer to these questions—was the program well designed, adequately resourced, and does it work in practice—helps the DoJ determine what action it should take. Once this is settled, the DoJ has several options about how to deal with violators.

## D.N.D.—Other Enforcement Tools of the DoJ

In the world of Cyber Speak, the letters "D.N.D." can be abbreviations for "Drunk & Disorderly," "Dungeons & Dragons," or "Dunkin' Donuts." But in the world of criminal justice, they are nontrial resolutions that stand for [D]eclinations, [N]on-prosecution Agreements (NPAs), and [D]eferred Prosecution Agreements (DPAs). In an indirect way, this is like an organization hanging a D.N.D.—("Do Not Disturb")—sign on its door targeted toward the DoJ so the company can go back to doing business as usual.

DPAs, NPAs, and Declinations represent the "carrots" compared to the "sticks" of large fines and debarment from doing business with the U.S. government. To be considered for any of these alternatives, in "… addition to criminal and civil penalties, companies may also be required to forfeit the proceeds of their crimes, or disgorge the profits generated from the crimes."[4] The purpose behind disgorgement is to make sure the perpetrator doesn't profit by its misconduct. The violator should be placed in the same position it occupied before the crime was committed.

So, what is in it for the DoJ and VBLs? Why are they negotiating these agreements?

> For prosecutors, they offer a middle ground between a more lengthy and protracted investigation (and possible trial) and the lack of any enforcement. In turn, less time spent on a single case allows prosecutors to use their limited resources to investigate allegations of wrongdoing by others.
>
> For companies, the lack of a lengthy investigation and possible trial diminishes litigation-related expenses, promotes certainty in the end-result, and enables the company to focus on improving its compliance processes and internal controls to protect against future potential violations.[5]

In the spirit of compromise, both parties gain certainty, avoid lengthy litigation, and "… for companies, the resolution offered by a DP—(and even potentially an NPA)—mitigates at least somewhat the unwelcome distraction that a protracted investigation and prosecution could have on the company, including its reputation."[6]

### Monitors

One business consideration is whether the government will require a monitor to be appointed. These monitors are paid for by the offending organization and usually last between three and five years. Monitors are oftentimes former DoJ prosecutors who are now partners in large law firms. They act as a liaison between the government and the offending organization and oversee the implementation of the NPA or DPA. The monitor will also work with the values-based leaders to develop a more effective ethics and compliance program, along with better internal controls.

In 2021, the DoJ had a new sheriff in town. Deputy Attorney General Lisa Monaco took a very different approach to monitorships from the previous administration. In her October 28, 2021 speech to the American Bar Association, she stated:

> In recent years, some have suggested that monitors would be the exception and not the rule. To the extent that prior Justice Department guidance suggested that monitorships are disfavored or are the exception, I am rescinding that guidance. Instead, I am making clear that the department is free to require the imposition of independent monitors whenever it is appropriate to do so in order to satisfy our prosecutors that a company is living up to its compliance and disclosure obligations under the DPA or NPA.[7]

Declinations, NPAs, DPAs, and Monitorships are powerful tools in the DoJ's fight against corruption, bribery, and other violations. The values-based leaders that receive the most favorable treatment will understand what the DoJ considers in making these decisions and incorporate them into their own compliance and ethics programs.

## Compliance Can Increase Revenue

In addition to reducing costs associated with potential litigation and a loss in reputation, compliance programs can also increase revenue, according to two researchers from Indiana University—Todd Haugh and Suneal Bedi. "Most simply put, extant work has largely been about how compliance programs can *save* companies money, whereas our study demonstrates that compliance programs can affirmatively *make* companies money."[8]

Using sophisticated marketing research tools, they focused on how consumers would be willing to pay more for products offered by companies with effectively designed compliance programs. Haugh and Bedi make the case that a compliance department should no longer be viewed as "the department of no," but as a revenue center and strategic business unit.

# Conclusion

According to the FSGO, an effective ethics and compliance program will promote "an organizational culture that encourages ethical conduct and a commitment to compliance with the law...."[9] Well-thought-out and implemented programs can decrease the number of violations and detect those it didn't prevent. In addition to having less misconduct, an effective program will be an important factor in how the DoJ treats a prospective defendant.

## Planning

To paraphrase a quote attributed to either Ben Franklin, Winston Churchill, Alan Lakein, or Serena and Venus Williams' father Richard— "Those who fail to plan, are planning to fail." Regardless of who originated it, this saying is a critically important step in developing effective ethics and compliance programs. But planning may not be enough. Values-based leaders must always be thinking, probing, monitoring, and evaluating all aspects of their compliance and ethics programs. VBLs should prepare for high-risk situations, but not lose sight of low risk, but high impact, difficult to predict "black swan" incidents. They need to build their plans to withstand the test of time under varying scenarios. To quote Mike Tyson—"Everyone's got a plan until they get punched in the mouth." Are VBLs' compliance and ethics plans ready to "get socked" by "Iron Mike"?

# Appendix I: *Goodco v. Badco Fine Range*

## *The Formula*

The USSC developed the equation for federal judges to apply in calculating how much an organization should pay for a violation. The first factor in the formula awarded victims restitution by disgorging the defendant's ill-gotten gains. Next, courts determine the base fine by using the greater of: (1) an Offense Level Table which could be increased or decreased by certain considerations, (2) the unlawful profits gained, or (3) pecuniary losses caused to others.[10] This Offense Level Table was established in FSGO §8C2.4(d), which is a chart starting with violations listed as level 6 or less. A level 6 crime would have a corresponding fine of $8,500. This progressed up to a level 38 offense, carrying a $150,000,000 initial penalty.

## *FSGO §8C2.4(d) Offense Level Table*

| Offense level | Amount of the fine |
| --- | --- |
| 6 or less | $8,500 |
| 7 | $15,000 |
| 8 | $15,000 |
| 9 | $25,000 |
| 10 | $35,000 |
| 11 | $50,000 |
| 12 | $70,000 |
| 13 | $100,000 |
| 14 | $150,000 |
| 15 | $200,000 |
| 16 | $300,000 |
| 17 | $450,000 |
| 18 | $600,000 |
| 19 | $850,000 |
| 20 | $1,000,000 |
| 21 | $1,500,000 |
| 22 | $2,000,000 |
| 23 | $3,000,000 |
| 24 | $3,500,000 |

*(Continues)*

(*Continued*)

| Offense level | Amount of the fine |
|---|---|
| 25 | $5,000,000 |
| 26 | $6,500,000 |
| 27 | $8,500,000 |
| 28 | $10,000,000 |
| 29 | $15,000,000 |
| 30 | $20,000,000 |
| 31 | $25,000,000 |
| 32 | $30,000,000 |
| 33 | $40,000,000 |
| 34 | $50,000,000 |
| 35 | $65,000,000 |
| 36 | $80,000,000 |
| 37 | $100,000,000 |
| 38 or more | $150,000,000 |

To determine the starting point for the table, violations were assigned "Base Level Offenses" in Chapter 2 of the Sentencing Guidelines Manual— (the section associated with Individual Offenders). Our hypothetical Goodco and Badco both had employees who paid a foreign official several bribes totaling $1,000,000 in order to secure a multimillion dollar contract for their company. This would be a violation of the FCPA addressed in §2C.1.1(a), which starts as a level 12 offense (14 if the defendant was a public official).[11] This offense level is then increased by other factors including: (1) add two levels if the offense involved more than one bribe, (2) if the amount of payment made to the public official, the benefit received by the defendant, or the loss to the government, exceeded $6,500 increase by the number of levels from the table in §2B.1.1 dealing with fraud:[12]

### §2B.1.1—Specific Offense Characteristics

| Loss (apply the greatest) | Increase in level |
|---|---|
| $6,500 | No increase |
| More than $6,500 | Add 2 |
| More than $15,000 | Add 4 |
| More than $40,000 | Add 6 |
| More than $95,000 | Add 8 |

| Loss (apply the greatest) | Increase in level |
|---|---|
| More than $150,000 | Add 10 |
| More than $250,000 | Add 12 |
| More than $550,000 | Add 14 |
| More than $1,500,000 | Add 16 |
| More than $3,500,000 | Add 18 |
| More than $9,500,000 | Add 20 |
| More than $25,000,000 | Add 22 |
| More than $65,000,000 | Add 24 |
| More than $150,000,000 | Add 26 |
| More than $250,000,000 | Add 28 |
| More than $550,000,000 | Add 30 |

and finally (3) add four levels if the offense involved a public official.[13]

What is the formula for the next data point of the penalty for our hypothetical Goodco and Badco for each $1,000,000 bribe?

| | |
|---|---|
| Base level offense for a bribe | = level 12 violation |
| More than one bribe | = add 2 levels |
| Profit/Bribe between $550,000 and $1.5 million | = add 14 levels |
| Involving public official in high level position | = add 4 levels |
| Adjusted Offense Level | = 32 |
| §8C2.4(d) Offense Level Table base fine subject to culpability score = $30,000,000 | |

This base fine is then increased or decreased by the organization's blameworthiness using a "Culpability Score." Each score has a minimum multiplier and a maximum multiplier, which is twice the amount of the minimum. Just like in golf, once you're playing the game, the goal is to get the smallest tally possible. All criminal offenses start with a score of "5" and are increased by the following factors. Add five points if the organization, or a unit of the organization, had 5,000 or more employees, involved high-level personnel, and tolerance of the offense by substantial authority personnel was pervasive. Under similar circumstances, but with an organization or unit with 1,000 or more employees—add 4 points to the score.[14] Companies with 200 or more employees would add 3 points. With 50 or more employees, add 2 points and a small company with 10 or more employees would add 1 point.

Culpability scores were not just limited to increases for higher fines. A violator could shave three strokes from their scorecard if it had an effective compliance and ethics program. This subtotal could be reduced by up to eight points for organizations that voluntarily disclosed the violation to the government, cooperated in the investigation, and accepted responsibility for its actions. If the company didn't voluntarily disclose the violation but did cooperate and accepted responsibility, it could receive a two-point deduction.

*Culpability Score*

| Culpability score | Minimum multiplier | Maximum multiplier |
|---|---|---|
| 10 or more | 2.00 | 4.00 |
| 9 | 1.80 | 3.60 |
| 8 | 1.60 | 3.20 |
| 7 | 1.40 | 2.80 |
| 6 | 1.20 | 2.40 |
| 5 | 1.00 | 2.00 |
| 4 | 0.80 | 1.60 |
| 3 | 0.60 | 1.20 |
| 2 | 0.40 | 0.80 |
| 1 | 0.20 | 0.40 |
| 0 or less | 0.05 | 0.20 |

Let's return to our hypothetical FCPA violations. For Badco, the company had 5,000 employees, the briber was a high-level person, and people with substantial authority knew about and tolerated the offense. Here is how their culpability score would be calculated:

| | |
|---|---|
| Starting point | = 5 |
| 5,000 or more employees and (1) high-level personnel participated in condoning or were willfully ignorant of the offense, or (2) there was pervasive tolerance of the offense by personnel with substantial authority | = add 5 points |
| Culpability score | = 10 points |
| Minimum and maximum multiplier | = 2.0–4.0 |
| Applying the multiplier range of 2.0–4.0 to a base fine of $30,000,000, the fine range should be between $60,000,000 and $120,000,000. | |

How would this apply to Goodco? While Goodco did have more than 5,000 employees, senior management was unaware of the bribery. It voluntarily self-disclosed, had an effective ethics and compliance program, cooperated with the government investigation, and accepted responsibility for its mistakes.

| Starting point | = 5 |
|---|---|
| Had an effective compliance program, cooperated with the government investigation, and accepted responsibility for its actions | = subtract 8 points |
| Culpability score | = 0 points |
| Minimum and maximum multiplier | = 0.05–0.20 |
| Applying the multiplier range of 0.05–0.20 to a base fine of $30,000,000, the fine range should be between $1,500,000 and $6,000,000. | |
| Applying DoJ 9-47.120—FCPA Corporate Enforcement Policy, companies that voluntarily self-disclosed, fully cooperate, and remediate can qualify for a 75 percent reduction off the low end of the fine range, bringing the new range from $375,000 to $1,500,000. | |

With a potential $120,000,000 fine for Badco and a possible $375,000 sanction for Goodco, the risk–reward calculus has changed dramatically (320:1) after Chapter 8 of the U.S. Sentencing Guidelines was adopted on November 1, 1991.

# Appendix II—Declinations, Deferred Prosecution Agreements, and Nonprosecution Agreements

## Declinations

No company wants to be prosecuted by the DoJ for possible criminal violations. If the Department begins an investigation, the organization can try to convince them to drop it. This exercise of "negative discretion" by the prosecutor is known as a "declination." "Declinations with Disgorgement are a new resolution option developed by the DoJ through the FCPA Pilot Program, which was formalized as the FCPA Corporate Enforcement Policy in November 2017 (Justice Manual 9-47.120)."[15] These are negotiated letter agreements counter-signed by the company that typically involve disgorgement, admissions, and continuing cooperation. Depending on how the violator reacts to the investigation, there can be a presumption that the DoJ will decline prosecution.

> When a company has voluntarily self-disclosed misconduct in an FCPA matter, fully cooperated, and timely and appropriately remediated, all in accordance with the standards set forth below, there will be a presumption that the company will receive a declination absent aggravating circumstances involving the seriousness of the offense or the nature of the offender.[16]

## Case Study 5.2—Dun & Bradstreet's Declination

One example of a declination occurred on April 23, 2018, when the DoJ granted Dun & Bradstreet—(D&B)—their request regarding an FCPA violation by one of its Chinese subsidiaries—Huaxia Dun & Bradstreet Business Information Consulting Co., Limited—(HDBC).[17] Between 2006 and 2012, HDBC made illegal payments to Chinese officials to obtain information that would typically only be available to Chinese law enforcement, their Judiciary, and law firms representing clients in lawsuits. It was the type of data that would have been extremely beneficial to D&B's customers. While the violations were occurring, D&B failed to devise and maintain adequate internal controls to detect and prevent improper payments. HDBC mistakenly thought that if it used a third party to bribe the Chinese officials, HDBC and D&B would be shielded from liability.

Once VBLs at D&B investigated the violation, their actions were like "Goodco" addressed in a previous section of this chapter. Due to its values-based behavior, D&B received very favorable treatment from the DoJ:

> Based upon the information known to the Department at this time, we have declined prosecution consistent with the FCPA Corporate Enforcement Policy. We have reached this conclusion despite the bribery committed by employees of the Company's subsidiaries in China. We based this decision on a number of factors, including but not limited to: the fact that the Company identified the misconduct; the Company's prompt voluntary self-disclosure; the thorough investigation undertaken by the Company; its full cooperation in this matter, including identifying all individuals involved in or responsible for the misconduct, providing the Department all facts relating to that misconduct, making current and former employees available for interviews, and translating foreign language documents to English; the steps that the Company has taken to enhance its compliance program and its internal accounting controls; the Company's full remediation, including terminating the employment of 11 individuals involved in the China misconduct, including an officer of the China subsidiary and other senior employees of one subsidiary, and disciplining other employees by reducing bonuses, reducing salaries, lowering performance reviews, and formally reprimanding them; and the fact that the Company will be disgorging to the SEC the full amount of disgorgement as determined by the SEC.[18]

Complete transparency, prompt voluntary self-disclosure, and full cooperation will be key considerations for a coveted declination. Aggravating factors that will move the department toward an "inclination" to prosecute include: (1) whether senior management of the company was involved, (2) how much profit the organization made off the misconduct,

(3) how pervasive was the misconduct, and (4) had it done similar deeds in the past (recidivism).[19]

### Nonprosecution Agreement—(NPA)

Prior to 2004, the DoJ's choices regarding organizational misconduct were binary—charge or don't charge. In 2003, then Deputy Attorney General—("DAG")—Larry Thompson gave federal prosecutors a third option—"alternative resolution vehicles"—in the form of NPAs and DPAs.[20] Before that time, NPAs had only been applied to individuals, not organizations.

NPAs are agreements between the department and the defendant that could be made public but aren't filed with the court; therefore, there was no judicial scrutiny and oversight.

> Thus, there is no independent review to determine if evidence exists to support the essential elements of the "crime" not prosecuted or to determine whether valid and legitimate defenses are relevant to the alleged conduct. In other words, when utilizing an NPA, the DOJ occupies the role of prosecutor, judge, and jury all at the same time.[21]

The 2003 "Thompson Memo" was modified in 2008 by then DAG—Mark Filip. The "Filip Memo" would formalize the use of DPAs and NPAs as the third choice for prosecutors:

> In certain instances, it may be appropriate . . . to resolve a corporate criminal case by means other than indictment. Non-prosecution and deferred prosecution agreements, for example, occupy an important middle ground between declining prosecution and obtaining the conviction of a corporation.[22]

The DoJ retained significant leverage over defendants who didn't want to risk prolonged litigation. In return, DPAs and NPAs, especially regarding FCPA violations can make it easier for the DoJ to process and close a higher volume of cases.

Former DoJ Attorney General Alberto Gonzales commented that it is "easy, much easier quite frankly" for the DoJ to resolve FCPA inquiries with NPAs and DPAs and that alternative resolution vehicles have "less of a toll" on the DoJ's budget and "provide revenue" to the DoJ.[23]

"Providing revenue" through FCPA settlements might be an understatement. "Many of these are 'cash cow' cases for Justice.... It's a government program that is profitable to the U.S. Treasury."[24]

## Case Study 5.3—Legg Mason and Nonprosecution Agreements—(NPA)

A June 4, 2018 case against Legg Mason is an example of an NPA.[25] Between 2004 and 2010, a subsidiary—(or agent)—of Legg Mason—Permal—partnered with Société Générale—(SG)—to solicit business in Libya. SG paid bribes through a Libyan broker in connection with 14 investments made by Libyan state-owned banks. SG paid the broker over $90 million to secure investments from Libyan state institutions into SG. SG got 13 investments and one restructuring deal from Libyan state institutions approximating $3.66 billion, with profits of about $523 million. Legg Mason, through its subsidiary Permal, managed seven of the investments earning $31.6 million in profits.

In exchange for an NPA, Legg Mason agreed to pay $32.625 million as a penalty and a disgorgement of $31.6 million in illegal profits for a total payment of $64.2 million. Legg Mason agreed to cooperate with the Criminal Division Fraud Section of the DoJ, which is responsible for investigating and prosecuting all FCPA matters.[26]

The Department reached this resolution based on a number of factors, including that Legg Mason did not voluntarily and timely disclose the conduct at issue, but fully cooperated in the investigation and fully remediated. Moreover, Legg Mason's misconduct involved only mid-to-lower level employees of Permal, a subsidiary company, and was not pervasive throughout Legg Mason or Permal; Société Générale—and not Legg Mason or

Permal—maintained the relationship with the Libyan broker and was responsible for originating and leading the scheme; the profits earned by Legg Mason and Permal were less than one-tenth of the profits earned by Société Générale; and neither Legg Mason nor Permal has a history of similar misconduct.[27]

Legg Mason is an interesting example of when the department will engage in NPAs, but these agreements don't seem to be utilized as much as DPAs. "Of 2020's 38 total NPAs and DPAs, 9 are NPAs and 29 are DPAs."[28] This generated nearly $9.4 billion in recoveries for the government.[29]

### Deferred Prosecution Agreement—(DPA)

There are a number of differences between an NPA and a DPA. First, DPAs are filed in federal court, along with a charging document called a "criminal information." This means it is a public record and subject to judicial review. NPAs typically don't require the company to admit criminal liability, while DPAs require admissions sufficient to justify an indictment. DPAs oftentimes last for three years, and the charges are dismissed if the defendant satisfies all the terms of the agreement.

## Case Study 5.4—Goldman Sachs and a Deferred Prosecution Agreement

A landmark DPA occurred on October 22, 2020. Goldman Sachs and its Malaysian subsidiary—(GS Malaysia)—admitted to conspiring to violate the FCPA by giving bribes between 2009 and 2014.[30] This scheme revolved around paying over $1 billion in bribes to underwrite $6.5 billion in bond deals for 1 Malaysia Development Bhd.—(1MDB). Goldman Sachs earned hundreds of millions of dollars in fees from these deals and agreed to pay $2.9 billion as part of a global settlement. This represented criminal fines and disgorgement as part of a DPA with the DoJ. At the time, it was the largest criminal penalty paid to the United States for an FCPA violation.

There were a number of factors why Goldman Sachs didn't receive better treatment that could have been available under a DoJ declination or an NPA. The company didn't voluntarily disclose its misconduct, the scheme involved high-level company employees, the size of the bribes, and the positions of the foreign government officials who received them. Goldman only received a partial credit—(10 percent reduction)—for its incomplete cooperation with the investigation because it was slow to produce important documents.

Not only did this three-year DPA set a record-high fine for bribery, but the DoJ also incorporated many other conditions into the agreement. Goldman would have to agree to the Statement of Facts and that it would not dispute it in any subsequent litigation. If the department, in its sole discretion, determined that Goldman had violated any terms of the DPA, the DoJ could terminate the agreement entirely or add an additional one year to the DPA. Goldman also agreed to continue enhancing its compliance programs, internal controls, and anticorruption training.

# LESSON 6

# What Happens if an Individual Gets in Trouble?

Leaders should understand the history and ramifications of white-collar crime. What happens if values-based leaders (VBLs) or their associates get caught up in criminal activity? This chapter discusses how white-collar criminals were treated before the Federal Sentencing Guidelines for Individuals were passed in 1987. Prior to that time, federal judges had a great deal of discretion in sentencing. In response to sentencing disparity, Congress passed the Sentencing Reform Act in 1984, which established the United States Sentencing Commission—(USSC). The USSC was charged with making recommendations to Congress about sentencing ranges for a variety of federal offenses. These guidelines came under attack, and the 2005 U.S. Supreme Court decisions of Booker and Fanfan restored some sentencing discretion to judges.

The second part of the chapter analyzes Bernie Madoff's Ponzi scheme. What led to his behavior and how was he treated at trial? It concludes with discussing his 150-year prison sentence and his life and death in a federal penitentiary in Butner, North Carolina.

# #6—"Nothing Focuses the Mind Like the Prospect of a Hanging"—Samuel Johnson

## Introduction

The previous lesson analyzed how values-based leaders could help their organizations qualify for significant fine reductions, declinations, nonprosecution agreements, and deferred prosecution agreements—also known as "Pre-trial Diversions." On September 9, 2015, then Deputy Attorney General—(DAG)—Sally Yates—sent a memo to the members of the Department of Justice clarifying what companies needed to do to receive this favorable treatment. The "Yates Memo" stated: "To be eligible for any cooperation credit, corporations must provide to the Department all relevant facts about the individuals involved in corporate misconduct."[1] Companies could no longer protect senior executives, if they wanted favorable treatment. Values-based leaders would have to work with the DoJ to hold their white-collar criminal associates accountable. Different DAGs have taken varied approaches to a company's need to "give up" these leaders. Prudent officials shouldn't bet their liberty, hoping for a lenient application of this standard.

This chapter answers three questions:

1. Where did the concept of white-collar crime come from?
2. How was it addressed by the USSC?
3. How was it applied to Bernie Madoff?

## A Catchphrase Enters the Business Vocabulary

In 1939, sociologist Edwin H. Sutherland created a new term for corporate misconduct—"white collar crime." His original definition described it as a "crime committed by a person of respectability and high social status in the course of his occupation."[2] This explanation was refined by Herbert Edelhertz who dropped Sutherland's emphasis on prestige and gender by focusing on the offense, not the offender. Edelhertz described white-collar crime as "an illegal act or series of illegal acts committed by nonphysical means and by concealment or guile, to obtain money or property, to avoid payment or loss of money or property, or to obtain business or personal advantage."[3] Now that the act is defined, how is it applied to the actors?

### Indeterminate Sentencing

In 2020, Otto Law wrote, "Here is a riddle: one man steals $100 in quarters, while another hides millions of dollars from the IRS. What's the same in the two cases? The answer, frequently, is the sentence."[4] Before the U.S. Sentencing Guidelines were enacted in 1987, federal judges could impose almost any sentence authorized by law. These terms weren't subject to review. During this time, not all defendants, regardless of the color of their collar, received similar treatment. Sentencing could play out very differently between two adjudicators.

> In addition, because each judge functionally operated as a law unto himself or herself, identical defendants—appearing before different judges—could receive wildly different punishments. Thus, a defendant in one courtroom might be sentenced to a lengthy prison term; whereas in the courtroom next door, an identical defendant, convicted of the same crime, might receive only probation.[5]

How did this apply to business misconduct by those who stole with a pen or computer instead of a gun or knife? Some said, "white-collar crime got white-collar time," meaning not much if any prison sentence. Congress understood that economic criminals often received lenient sentences.

> The Senate Report on the SRA (Sentencing Reform Act) indicated that too many white-collar offenders were given probation "without due consideration given to the fact that the heightened deterrent effect of incarceration and the readily perceivable receipt of just punishment accorded by incarceration were of critical importance."[6]

If convicted, these "Masters of the Universe" had public relations firms rebranding their images from greedy lawbreakers into philanthropic pillars of the community. To minimize the time for the crime, they would provide the court boxes brimming with glowing testimonials from politicians to celebrities, extolling their misunderstood friend's virtuous deeds and charitable activities. These business bandits might expect a slap on their wrists, possibly followed by a slap on their back as they left the courtroom. "See you at the club, your honor."

## A Commission Is Commissioned

This seemingly random sentencing "roulette" instead of a predictable "rubric" was one of the motivating factors behind two former giants of the Senate—Strom Thurmond and Ted Kennedy—coming together to champion the Federal Sentencing Guidelines. They both advanced the concept of sentencing reform, but their motives were very different. "Ted Kennedy was concerned that too many poor people, too many minorities got unduly harsh sentences.... Strom Thurmond was concerned that there were too many liberal lenient judges who let people off easy."[7] It may have been one of the few times in recorded Congressional history that Senators Thurmond and Kennedy ever agreed on anything, but they settled on punishing offenders based on the crime, not which judge heard the case. Brinksmanship was replaced by statesmanship. A spirit of civility and compromise countered courtroom chaos, which led to the passage of the Sentencing Reform Act (SRA) of 1984. Unfortunately, this type of cooperation has rarely been a guiding principle since then.

The USSC was created by the SRA of 1984. The original group of seven commissioners included then Circuit Judge for the U.S. Court of Appeals for the First Circuit and future Supreme Court Associate Justice—Stephen Breyer. Breyer noted the previous problems parole posed in predictable imprisonment. Pre-Guidelines, federal judges knew that the Parole Board was allowed to release defendants after only serving about one-third of their sentence. This could lead to judicial "gamesmanship" and even more variable sentences. "With sentencing authority divided between the judge and the United States Parole

Commission, some judges attempted to craft sentences to anticipate the decisions of the Parole Commission, while others did not."[8] Since the Guidelines eliminated parole, federal offenders would now serve at least 85 percent of their original sentence. The best they could hope for was the 54 days per year of "good time," which could be forfeited for any "bad times" they were involved in at their prison. Instead of indeterminant sentencing, defendants would now be punished according to their previous criminal history (six different columns), if any, along with 43 rows of an "Offense Level Table" determined by the severity of their misconduct.

These 258 separate cells—(matrix grid, not prison)—contained a narrow—low to high—range of months that would force the judge's sentencing decision into a small box. This took away much of their judicial discretion to consider factors not included in the Guidelines' rubric. But discretion is like energy or hydraulics. It "can never be extinguished; it is simply dislodged and shifted to other system parts."[9] In this case, power moved to prosecutors whose charging decisions put tremendous pressure on defendants to accept plea agreements that seemed harsher than those meted out pre-Guidelines.

### Judicial Discretion Restored?

"The Sentencing Guidelines have been misnamed since their inception. They act as mandates on sentencing courts, vastly restricting discretion."[10] This may have been true between 1987 and 2005, but several Supreme Court decisions restored some power to judges. "In a 5-4 vote in *United States v. Booker* and *United States v. Fanfan*, the justices ruled that the sixth amendment right to a jury trial requires that current federal sentencing guidelines be advisory, not mandatory."[11] After these rulings, judges would still need to calculate and reference the relevant guidelines sentencing ranges but were no longer bound to follow them.

Sentencing was almost back where it started—"from total discretion, to mandatory guidelines with virtually no discretion, to advisory guidelines with considerable discretion."[12] How would these revised guidelines be applied to one of the worst white-collar criminals in history?

# Case Study 6.1—The Rise and Fall of Bernie Madoff

Bernard L. Madoff provides a cautionary tale for all values-based leaders. At one point in his career, he might have had principles, but quickly lost his way. Madoff was born on April 29, 1938. His humble upbringing wasn't the traditional route to success on Wall Street. Without family connections, networking at elite universities, or access to intergenerational wealth, Madoff would appear to be shut out and thought, "I was upset with the whole idea of not being in the club. I was this little Jewish guy from Brooklyn."[13] As a 22-year-old, he founded the Bernard L. Madoff Investment Securities—(BLMIS)—in 1960 and started with his $500 life savings.

Madoff made a living in the early years of BLMIS by making the trades too small for industry giants like Goldman Sachs and Bear Stearns to bother with.

> "I was perfectly happy to take the crumbs," he said. Madoff was a market-maker, a middleman between those who wanted to buy and sell small quantities of mostly bonds—odd lots. "It was a riskless business," he said. "You made the spread," buying at one price and selling at a higher one, and in those days the spreads could be substantial, 50 or 75 cents or even a dollar a share.[14]

Madoff's reputation and influence grew over the years, and he was the Chairman of the National Association of Securities Dealers Automated Quotations—(NASDAQ)—in 1990, 1991, and 1993. In addition to BLMIS, Madoff opened an advisory business, operating on a different floor of the Lipstick Building and was totally separated from the securities firm. These advisory business records were kept under lock and key to avoid the prying eyes of family members and regulators. This is where Madoff hatched the idea of the "split-strike conversion strategy." He promised it would bring huge returns, consistently making substantial profits in both bear and bull markets. This scheme involved:

> "...a long equity position plus a long put and a short call."

If that confuses you, don't worry it is supposed to, and it explains

why so many people—including celebrities and some sophisticated investors—had no idea they were investing in the world's
largest Ponzi scheme.[15]

It didn't matter whether they understood what happened inside this
financial "black box." It all came down to just "trust Bernie."

## Ponzi's Polygon

The "split-strike conversion" did not work, so Madoff reverted to a
simpler strategy—lying. He followed the lead of the original financial pyramid schemer—Charles Ponzi. In 1920, Ponzi convinced
thousands of Bostonians they could earn a 50 percent return on their
investment within 45 days. His strategy involved international postal
coupons, which could be purchased inexpensively in countries with
weak economies and then exchanged for U.S. postage stamps for a significant profit. It was an interesting idea but didn't work in practice.
Ponzi paved the way for future fraudsters, including Madoff, to make
massive mounds of money. Pay off old investors with money from new
ones—(and skim off a healthy percentage to buy luxurious properties
including a Manhattan penthouse, along with vacation homes on the
French Riviera, Palm Beach, and Montauk, Long Island). New investors
would see satisfied customers and pour more money into the black box
or black hole. This scheme worked as long as an exponentially greater
number of new victims kept flowing in.

Madoff followed this playbook by promising investors high rates of
return, but all he did was use perfect hindsight to reverse engineer and
calculate the imaginary gains.

> (Madoff) used to keep boxes of old Wall Street Journals and they
> would take the stock tables, stock prices that were published every
> day at the time and they would just lay them out, end to end on
> the floor … [with] 10, 20 30 feet of newspapers, side to side. And
> so you'd sit in an office chair that had wheels, a wheeled chair, and
> you'd sort of slide from left to right to pick the right day with the
> right stock with the right price.[16]

Madoff didn't execute any of these trades. His office merely reported the fictional gains as real, and his clients were gullible enough to believe them.

Madoff had some partners—(or at least associates)—in crime. Two of his computer programmers—George Perez and Jerry O'Hara—wrote the code that generated the sham transactions for the clueless clients.

> According to the complaint, the coders created books and records to hide the scope and nature of the business; changed the names of account holders to support fraudulent activity; and altered details about share and equities transactions, including creating fictitious times for the transactions and generating fraudulent documents to make it appear that the investment firm was buying and selling securities on the London Stock Exchange.[17]

After a while, these programmers realized the scheme was a scam and confronted one of Madoff's lieutenants—Frank DiPascali. DiPascali alerted Madoff about the programmer's problems, and Madoff told DiPascali to give them whatever they asked for to keep them quiet. The programmers wanted to be paid in diamonds to limit any paper trail. DiPascali's response was—"Where the hell am I gonna get a bag of diamonds."[18] DiPascali ultimately paid them between $60,000 and $64,000 apiece in cash, and the programmers continued working in the firm until Madoff was arrested on December 11, 2008. In 2014, both Perez and Ohara received 2.5-year prison sentences for their role in the fraud.

Clients didn't spot the red flags that Madoff's returns were too good to be true, being "in the green" (profitable) more than 90 percent of the time. The only "red" they saw was when the unbelievable returns didn't quite reach their unrealistic expectations.

> The forgeries committed on some clients' documents, Fishman said, were even done as if to order by some clients. According to ex-FBI agent Steve Garfinkel, Annette Bongiorno, Madoff's longtime assistant and first employee, would doctor statements on request. Clients would call to complain that Madoff promised

18 percent but they'd gotten 16 percent. Bongiorno would respond with an amended statement showing the promised rate.[19]

While the prosecutor wanted Bongiorno to spend more time in jail, in 2014, she was sentenced to six years in prison. If it was any consolation to victims, U.S. District Judge Laura Taylor Swain also held Bongiorno jointly liable, along with the other Madoff co-conspirators, to repay $155 billion.

### The Ponzi Scheme Debunked

While Steven Spielberg, Larry King, Kevin Bacon and his wife Kyra Sedgwick, NY Mets owner—Fred Wilpon, and the Elie Wiesel Foundation may have just "trusted Bernie," a Certified Fraud Examiner from Boston named Harry Markopolos did the math and determined "Emperor Bernie" had no clothes. Markopolos stated Madoff's "… strategy as depicted would have trouble beating a zero return, and his performance chart went up at a 45-degree line: that line doesn't exist in finance, it only exists in geometry classes."[20] In 2000, Markopolos sent his findings and concerns to the Boston Regional Office of the SEC but was told, "Madoff is headquartered in New York. It's not our jurisdiction. So I'm (Boston SEC) going to refer it to New York."[21] According to Markopolos, the investigation stalled there because "the relationship between the SEC's Boston and New York offices is about as warm and cordial as the Yankees-Red Sox rivalry."[22]

In 2006, the SEC did investigate Madoff and, during a deposition, asked him where he kept all the securities.

> Madoff said it was "amazing to me" that he didn't get caught during the Enforcement investigation, because they specifically asked him, "Are these securities at DTC (Depository Trust Company)?" They further pressed, "What is your account number." He replied, "646." … He went on to say that when they asked for the DTC account number, "I thought it was the end game, over. Monday morning they'll call DTC and this will be over … and it never happened."[23]

The SEC agents did contact the Depository Trust Company and verified Madoff had an account. Unfortunately, they didn't ask the follow-up question—"How much was in it?" Instead of billions, the account only contained $24 million. Madoff had bluffed his way through another investigation with deception, half-truths, and hiding the 4-foot tall "soft screw" polyurethane sculpture he kept on his credenza. This piece of art by Claes Oldenburg was valued at about $50,000, and Madoff used it to impress his visitors or maybe to intimidate them. Even though he personally dusted it, Madoff had enough sense to hide it during SEC investigations. Was the piece a metaphor for how Madoff treated his clients or an inside joke? Whatever the meaning, it was so potentially prejudicial that Judge Laura Taylor Swain demanded it be photoshopped out of pictures to be used during the subsequent fraud trial for one of Madoff's top employees—Daniel Bonventre. In 2014, even after images of "the soft screw" were erased, Bonventre was sentenced to "10 years in prison and financial penalties that will rob him of his ill-gotten wealth—a punishment that fits Bonventre's central role in the biggest financial fraud in history."[24]

### The Day of Reckoning

Ponzi schemes eventually collapse under their own weight. Madoff tried to delay this as long as possible by convincing his investors to keep their real money in his fake fund while sending them phony reports with their bogus earnings. The 2008 housing market collapse and subsequent recession caused many Bernie backers to request a redemption of their money. At that point, Madoff realized the game was over and on December 9, 2008, he confessed his sins to his brother and BLMIS Chief Compliance Officer—Peter Madoff. The next day, he repeated the story to his two sons—Mark and Andrew Madoff. On December 10, 2008, after consulting their attorneys, Mark and Andrew contacted the FBI and informed them about their father's fraud. On the morning of December 11, 2008, the FBI arrested Bernie Madoff in his pajamas.

Just over three months later, on March 12, 2009, Madoff—now dressed in a somber charcoal gray suit instead of his pj's—pleaded guilty to all 11 charges brought against him. These claims included securities fraud, mail fraud, wire fraud, money laundering, and perjury. If all the sentences were stacked together as the prosecutors requested, Madoff faced 150 years in prison. His actual sentence was in the hands of U.S. District Judge Denny Chin.

Madoff's attorney—Ira Sorkin—argued that the defendant would enter prison as a 71-year-old, with a life expectancy of 13 years. Twelve years would in effect become a life sentence, with the possibility of being released near the end of his life. Judge Chin wasn't satisfied with that request and posed the prison problem to his law clerks. They suggested he "split the baby" and sentence Madoff to 75 years. Judge Chin needed more than a compromise—he wanted a thoughtful rationale which would send an important message to Madoff and others.

One factor in the equation was the judge weighing the victim's statements from 450 e-mails he had received.

Judge Chin said he was particularly moved by an account of a man who had invested his life savings with Mr. Madoff, then died of a heart attack two weeks later. The man's widow had met with Mr. Madoff, who had put his arm around her and told her not to worry, that her money was safe with him. "She eventually gave him her own pension, 401(k) funds," Judge Chin wrote in his notes. He would include the story in his draft.[25]

The Judge also noted that he didn't receive any positive letters backing Madoff. "The absence of such support is telling."[26]

### Sentencing Rationales

When the SRA was passed in 1984, the USSC was directed to take the following sentencing purposes into account—retribution, deterrence, incapacitation, and rehabilitation. How would Judge Chin incorporate these theories into Bernard L. Madoff's prison time? "Rehabilitation" attempts to give inmates a new skill set or education to prepare them for an honest living, once released. This didn't really apply to Madoff. "Incapacitation" seems appropriate for dangerous felons we want to lock up as long as possible. There are pictures of the 70-year-old Bernie Madoff being escorted into court wearing a baseball cap covering his scruffy white hair. He may have been a scrappy septuagenarian, but most of his clients "could've taken him." He didn't seem scary. So much for incapacitation.

The two remaining sentencing theories Judge Chin did apply dealt with "deterrence" and "retribution." Chin wrote:

> Another important goal of punishment is deterrence, and the symbolism is important here because the strongest possible message must be sent to those who would engage in similar conduct that they will be caught and that they will be punished to the fullest extent of the law.[27]

Even two years after Judge Chin sentenced Madoff,

> [T]he judge, explaining why he had rejected the defense's request for a substantially shorter sentence, provided two reasons why the symbolism of a much longer term was important: to send the "strongest possible message" of deterrence, and to help the victims heal.[28]

Values-based leaders should note that the days of lenient sentences for white-collar criminals were over—at least for Bernie Madoff. Any future offenders would have to include this possibility into their corporate crime calculus.

"Retribution" is also known as "just desserts." Offenders should pay for the pain they've caused. Maybe the victims would get some satisfaction with a symbolically long sentence. Judge Chin wrote:

> In explaining how the 150-year sentence was symbolically important, he (Judge Chin) had neglected to include a third, crucial reason: retribution. "A defendant should get his just deserts," he remembered thinking. "One of the traditional notions of punishment," he wrote, "is that an offender should be punished in proportion to his blameworthiness." Mr. Madoff's crimes were "extraordinarily evil," he added. In a society governed by the rule

of law, he wrote, the message had to be sent that Mr. Madoff would "get what he deserves," and would be "punished according to his moral culpability."[29]

Steal $17.5 billion from investors and wind up spending 150 years in prison. That equates to 8.5 years for every billion dollars stolen. How sweet is that? (For a detailed analysis of how Judge Chin calculated Bernie Madoff's sentence, please see Appendix III.)

## Life in Prison

In his pre-prison days, one of Madoff's tougher fashion decisions might have been which one of his 46 high-end watches should he wear that day. Would it be Cartier or Rolex, or maybe it was just an ultracasual Swatch Day? His timepiece collection would be sold at auction to help repay his victims. One of the more expensive items was the 1945 Vintage Rolex Monoblocco chronograph wristwatch, which was sold at the Madoff auction for $65,000. It is a shame that Bernie couldn't keep this one since it was nicknamed "the prisoner's watch" because Rolex offered it to British Officers who were prisoners of war—(POWs)—during World War II. Since they were considered men of honor, these POWs could receive the watch while at the camp but pay for it when they returned home. The irony about Bernie Madoff and his fascination with watches is the last thing a person spending 150 years in prison needs to know is—"What time is it?"

Madoff wouldn't need a precision wristwatch to measure seconds, minutes, hours, days, months, years, decades, or centuries. His new life was filled with chores and just getting through the day:

> Madoff's former life of luxury will quickly turn into a life of rou-
> tine at Butner (federal prison in North Carolina.) Inmates start
> their day at 6 a.m. and are required to work 7.5 hours a day, as
> long as they're found medically fit, according to the Bureau of
> Prisons. Madoff will make between 12 cents and 40 cents an hour
> to be a groundskeeper, a food service employee or a commissary
> worker.[30]

Madoff sometimes forgot where he was and the fact that he no longer exercised power or control over others. "[O]ne interviewee recounts Madoff trying to change the television to a news report featuring his crimes while another inmate was watching something else. The other—much younger—man ended the dispute with 'an open-hand slap.'"[31]

Madoff did return to his entrepreneurial roots after working in the prison commissary.

> "Bernie really was a successful businessman with quite original insights into the market, and he's continued applying his business instincts in prison," Steve Fishman, the host of a new six-part series on Audible called "Ponzi Supernova" said in this Marketplace article. "At one point, he cornered the hot chocolate market. He bought up every package of Swiss Miss from the commissary and sold it for a profit in the prison yard. He monopolized hot chocolate! He made it so that, if you wanted any, you had to go through Bernie."[32]

One can imagine a 1920s prohibition era "speak easy," in which customers utter the secret password to get that sweet, warm drink. For all that effort, at least it should come with some marshmallows.

### Death in Prison

Madoff started his sentence as a 71-year-old. Even if he had received 20 years off his sentence for "good time" on his 200th birthday, Madoff would still have owed one more year before he would have been eligible for release. It turns out that Madoff's attorney's—Ira Sorkin—13-year prediction about his actuarial life expectancy was fairly accurate. Bernie Madoff died of kidney failure in prison on April 14, 2021.[33] All he had to show for his 12 years in prison was $710, "eight AAA batteries, four paperback religious books, a Casio calculator, four packages of popcorn, one package of ramen soup, a box of gefilte fish and not a whole lot more."[34] At that rate of earning about $0.24 per hour, it would have taken Bernie Madoff approximately 845 years to buy back his $50,000 "soft screw."

# Conclusion

Values-based leaders need to understand that their position within their companies and communities won't protect them against prosecution and prison. Rich and powerful principals may have access to good attorneys, but their celebrity status may also encourage the government to target them. A solid work ethic, combined with solid ethics, will be their best defense against charges of corruption.

# Appendix III—Calculating Bernie Madoff's Prison Sentence

So how did Judge Chin determine the 150-year sentence? None of the individual crimes carried a life sentence, but the statutory maximum sentences combined for the 11 charges added up to that amount:

## United States v. Bernard L. Madoff [35]

| Count | Charge | Maximum penalties in prison |
|-------|--------|------------------------------|
| One | Securities fraud | 20 years |
| Two | Investment advisor fraud | 5 years |
| Three | Mail fraud | 20 years |
| Four | Wire fraud | 20 years |
| Five | International money laundering to promote specified unlawful activity | 20 years |
| Six | International money laundering to conceal and disguise the proceeds of specified unlawful activity | 20 years |
| Seven | Money laundering | 10 years |
| Eight | False statements | 5 years |
| Nine | Perjury | 5 years |
| Ten | Making a false filing with the SEC | 20 years |
| Eleven | Theft from an employee benefit plan | 5 years |

Even though Madoff apologized to his victims stating, "I live in a tormented state now, knowing of all the pain and suffering that I have created,"[36] on June 29, 2009, Judge Denny Chin read the following passage in his courtroom:

> Mr. Madoff, please stand. It is the judgment of this Court that the defendant, Bernard L. Madoff, shall be and hereby is sentenced to a term of imprisonment of 150 years, consisting of 20 years on each of Counts 1, 3, 4, 5, 6, and 10, 5 years on each of Counts 2, 8, 9, and 11, and 10 years on Count 7, all to run consecutively to each other. As a technical matter, the sentence must be expressed on the judgment in months. 150 years is equivalent to 1,800 months.[37]

Just over two weeks later, on July 14, 2009, Madoff began the first day of his 1,800-month sentence at the Federal Correctional Complex in Butner, North Carolina.[38]

# Epilogue

Values-based leaders should heed these lessons regarding the life cycle of work. They have explored the positive and negative implications surrounding corporate culture, loyalty, motivations, whistleblowing, and white-collar crime for both organizations and individuals. The lessons have been peppered with anecdotal case studies from the business world and statistical evidence from the research world.

To put things in context and end on a more positive note, the book concludes with a poem by business ethicist—Michael Josephson entitled "What Will Matter." (Reprinted with permission from the author):

Ready or not, some day it will all come to an end.
There will be no more sunrises, no minutes, hours or days.
All the things you collected, whether treasured or forgotten
will pass to someone else.
Your wealth, fame and temporal power will shrivel to irrelevance.
It will not matter what you owned or what you were owed.
Your grudges, resentments, frustrations
and jealousies will finally disappear.
So too, your hopes, ambitions, plans and to-do lists will expire.
The wins and losses that once seemed so important will fade away.
It won't matter where you came from
or what side of the tracks you lived on at the end.
It won't matter whether you were beautiful or brilliant.
Even your gender and skin color will be irrelevant.
So what will matter?
How will the value of your days be measured?
What will matter is not what you bought
but what you built, not what you got but what you gave.
What will matter is not your success
but your significance.

What will matter is not what you learned
but what you taught.
What will matter is every act of integrity,
compassion, courage, or sacrifice
that enriched, empowered or encouraged others
to emulate your example.
What will matter is not your competence
but your character.
What will matter is not how many people you knew,
but how many will feel a lasting loss when you're gone.
What will matter is not your memories
but the memories that live in those who loved you.
What will matter is how long you will be remembered,
by whom and for what.
Living a life that matters doesn't happen by accident.
It's not a matter of circumstance but of choice.
Choose to live a life that matters.

# Notes

## Prologue

1. Copeland (2014).
2. Mayer, Davies, and Schoorman (1995), pp. 709–734.
3. McLain and Pendell (2023).
4. Deloitte (2021).
5. Used with permission from Procter & Gamble (n.d.).
6. Kanter and Bird (2009).
7. Pepper (2005).
8. Barnes (2001).

## Lesson 1

1. Gerstner (2003), pp. 181–182.
2. Memorandum (2006).
3. Smith (2012).
4. Treviño, Weaver, Gibson, and Toffler (1999), p.145.
5. Zappos (n.d.).
6. Nisen (2013).
7. Olson (2013).
8. Sandford (2018).
9. *L'Oréal Code of Ethics: The Way We Work* (n.d.).
10. Criminal Division of the U.S. Department of Justice and the Enforcement Division of the U.S. Securities and Exchange Commission (2020), p. 58.
11. Thornton (2019).
12. Treviño, Weaver, Gibson, and Toffler (1999), pp. 141–142.
13. Ibid, p. 143.
14. GE (n.d.).
15. Schwartz (2018).

16. Olson (2013), p. 18.
17. McClennan (2019).
18. Deloitte (2015).
19. Department of Health and Human Services: Office of Inspector General (n.d.).
20. Department of Health and Human Services: Office of Inspector General (1998).
21. U.S. Department of Justice Criminal Division: Evaluation of Corporate Compliance Programs (2023), p. 9.
22. U.S. Department of Justice Criminal Division: Evaluation of Corporate Compliance Programs (2020), pp. 1–2.
23. McClennan (2019).
24. Ethisphere (2020).
25. Ibid.
26. Walker and Soule (2017).
27. Groysberg, Lee, Price, and Cheng (2018).
28. Samuel (2020).
29. Ethisphere (2019).
30. Ibid.
31. Filabi and Bulgarella (2018), p. 5.
32. Scudamore (2016).
33. Kelly (2017).
34. Tedlow and Smith (2005).
35. Knight (1982).
36. Kimes (2010).
37. Kenvue (n.d.).
38. Koppel (1998).

# Lesson 2

1. Clifton (2023).
2. Greenleaf (2022).
3. Keeley (2022).
4. Ibid.
5. Ito (2022).
6. Terkel (1974), p. 405.

7. Buckingham (2022).

8. Molla (2022).

9. Tsipursky (2022).

10. Bindley (2021).

11. Oliver (2021).

12. Ibid.

13. Deczynski (2021).

14. Oliver (2021).

15. Ibid.

16. Feintzeig (2021).

17. Segal (2021).

18. Borchers (2022).

19. Ibid.

20. Sherman and Whitten (2023).

21. Tsipursky (2023).

22. Borchers (2022).

23. Tsipursky (2023).

24. Borchers (2022).

25. Parsi (2022).

26. Molla (2022).

27. Nguyen (2022).

28. Marks (2022).

29. Vozza (2022).

30. Liu (2021).

31. Bellace (2022).

32. Pendell (2022).

33. Harter (2023), p. 2.

34. Schatz (2022).

35. Ellis and Yang (2022).

36. IMDb—Page for *Office Space* (1991).

37. Clifton (2022).

38. IMDb—Page for *Office Space* (1991).

39. Hickman and Pietrocini (2019).

40. Pendell (2022).

41. Carlson (2013).

42. Choo (2023).

43. Southern (2023).
44. IMDb—Page for *The Company Men* (2010).
45. Gibbs (2022).
46. Maruf (2021).
47. Lufkin (2022).
48. Peterson (2020).
49. Cole (n.d.).
50. Buckingham (2022).
51. Ibid.
52. Parsi (2022).

## Lesson 3

1. Gaul (2013).
2. Twitter (2022).
3. *Ethics Unwrapped* (n.d.).
4. Lefcoe (1998), A14; This case can also be found in, Jennings (2018), p. 192.
5. I asked the student for permission to use this quote. I explained I would not refer to her name, company, or any other identifying features. I have substituted the word "factor," for a term that could identify her company. She gave me permission to use this quote.
6. Prentice (2015),p. 57; *citing* MacFarquhar (2012).
7. Belsky (2012).
8. Associated Press (2007).
9. IMDb's Page for *Snake Eyes* (1998).
10. IMDb Quotes—Page for *Boiler Room* (2000).
11. Marks (2012), p. 33.
12. Ibid.
13. Flitter (2020).
14. Egan (2016).
15. Olson (2013), p. 13.
16. Ibid, p. 15.
17. Internet Movie Script Database (IMSDb), page for *A Few Good Men* (1991).
18. Ibid.

19. Ibid.

20. IMDb, *A Few Good Men* (1991).

21. IMSDb, page for *A Few Good Men* (1991).

22. Schulweis (2010), p. 106.

23. Milgram (1974), p. 4.

24. Schulmann (2014), p. 426.

25. Pearlstein (2021).

26. NPR (2012).

27. Haugh (n.d.).

28. Bucy, Formby, Raspanti, and Rooney (2008), p. 401.

29. Prentice (2015), pp. 52–53.

# Lesson 4

1. Larmer (1992), p. 126; *citing* Bok (1988), pp. 261–262.

2. Ibid, p. 127; *citing* Near and Miceli (1985), p. 10.

3. Horwitz (2021),

4. Ibid.

5. Rowland (2020).

6. Sandburg (1954), p. 278.

7. Doyle (2021).

8. Bergman (n.d.).

9. Groenewald (2022), p. 23.

10. "Americans Who Tell the Truth" (n.d.).

11. Chambers (2022).

12. Ripley (2002).

13. *The Financial Express* (2010).

14. Retaliating Against a Witness, Victim or Informant, 18 U.S. Code §1513(e) (2023).

15. S. Rep. No. 107-146, at 10 (2002), www.congress.gov/congressional-report/107th-congress/senate-report/146/1.

16. Moberly (2007), p. 67.

17. Prager (2013), p. 25.

18. Morgenson (2011).

19. Baily, Litan, and Johnson (2008), p. 8.

20. Ramirez (2019), p. 620.

21. U.S. Securities and Exchange Commission (2020).
22. The Dodd Frank Act, §922(c)(1)(i)(II).
23. U.S. Securities and Exchange Commission (Press Release) (2021).
24. Gibeaut (2006).
25. Mathiason and Weindling (2005).
26. Ibid.
27. Henriksson and Stappers (2022).
28. Stappers (2022).
29. Carino, Menor, and Kaplan (2021).
30. Ibid.
31. Armenakis (2002), p. 277.
32. Frahrenthold (2014).
33. Riley and Iyengar (2018).
34. Woodford (2014), p. 111.
35. Detert (2018).

# Lesson 5

1. Storbeck (2023).
2. Deputy Attorney General Lisa O. Monaco Delivers Remarks on Corporate Criminal Enforcement (2022).
3. Millman (2013).
4. Criminal Division of the U.S. Department of Justice and the Enforcement Division of the U.S. Securities and Exchange Commission (2020), p. 71.
5. *Dow Jones* (n.d.).
6. Ibid.
7. Deputy Attorney General Lisa O. Monaco Gives Keynote Address at ABA's 36th National Institute on White Collar Crime, Department of Justice News (2021).
8. Haugh and Bedi (n.d.).
9. §8B2.1(b), United States Sentencing Commission Guidelines Manual (2018).
10. §8C2.4(a)(3), United States Sentencing Commission Guidelines Manual (2018).
11. §2C.1.1(a)(2), United States Sentencing Commission Guidelines Manual (2018).

12. §2C.1.1(b)(2), United States Sentencing Commission Guidelines Manual (2018).

13. §2C.1.1(b)(3), United States Sentencing Commission Guidelines Manual (2018).

14. §8C2.5(b)(2)(A)(i)-(ii), Involvement in or Tolerance of Criminal Activity, United States Sentencing Commission Guidelines Manual (2018).

15. Dunn (2020), p. 7.

16. 9-47.120—FCPA Corporate Enforcement Policy (2019).

17. April 23, 2018 Letter from the Department of Justice, Criminal Division, Fraud Section to Hogan Lovells, law firm representing The Dun & Bradstreet Corporation (2021).

18. Ibid.

19. Criminal Division of the U.S. Department of Justice and the Enforcement Division of the U.S. Securities and Exchange Commission (2020).

20. Koehler (2015).

21. Ibid.

22. Ibid; *citing* Memorandum from Mark Filip, Deputy Att'y Gen. (2008), p. 18.

23. Ibid; *citing* Koehler(2013).

24. Wayne (2012).

25. Department of Justice, Office of Public Affairs (2018).

26. Ibid.

27. Ibid.

28. Dunn (2021).

29. Ibid.

30. Department of Justice, Office of Public Affairs (2020).

# Lesson 6

1. Memorandum by Sally Quillian Yates (2015).

2. Sutherland (1949), p. 9.

3. Edelhertz (1970), p. 3.

4. Otto.Law (2020).

5. Vance (2019).

6. Bennett, Levinson, and Hioki (2017), p. 939.

7. Savage (2004).
8. *Testimony December 14, 1995 Richard P. Conaboy Chairman United States Sentencing Commission House Judiciary Crime Sentencing Commission, Federal Document Clearing House Congressional Testimony* (1995).
9. Vance (2019).
10. Keneally (2004), p. 46.
11. Mauro (2005).
12. Bennett, Levinson, and Hioki (2017), p. 939.
13. Fishman (2011).
14. Ibid.
15. "Madoff's Marvelous Returns: We Explore the Investment Returns Behind the World's Largest Ever Ponzi Scheme" (2017).
16. "The Rise and Fall of Madoff's Ponzi Scheme" (2021).
17. Zetter (2009).
18. "Ex-Madoff Programmers Wanted Payment in Diamonds, U.S. Jury Told" (2013).
19. Thielman (2017).
20. "Madoff Whistleblower: SEC Failed to Do the Math" (2010).
21. "Investigation of Failure of the SEC to Uncover Bernard Madoff's Ponzi Scheme—Public Version" (2009), pp. 64–65.
22. Carozza (2009).
23. "Investigation of Failure of the SEC to Uncover Bernard Madoff's Ponzi Scheme—Public Version" (2009), p. 312.
24. "Former Director of Operations for Bernard L. Madoff Investment Securities, Daniel Bonventre, Sentenced in Manhattan Federal Court to 10 Years in Prison for His Role in the Massive Fraud" (2014).
25. Weiser (2011).
26. Ibid.
27. United States of America v. Bernard L. Madoff, Sentencing by Judge Denny Chin, 96TJMADF, 09 CR 213 (DC) (2009), pp. 47–48.
28. Weiser (2011).
29. Ibid.
30. Chuchmach, Esposito, and Katersky (2009).
31. Thielman (2017).
32. Mark (2017).

33. Reimann (2021).

34. Mangan (2021).

35. *Bernard L. Madoff Pleads Guilty to 11-Count Criminal Information and Is Remanded Into Custody (2009).*

36. Henriques (2009).

37. Judge Denny Chin, Sentencing Bernard L. Madoff, Statement by Judge Denny Chin, (p. 49 lines 14–22) 96TJMADF, 09 CR 213 (DC) (2009).

38. Chuchmach, Esposito, and Katersky (2009).

# References

"Americans Who Tell the Truth." n.d. www.americanswhotellthetruth.org/portraits/coleen-rowley.

"Ex-Madoff Programmers Wanted Payment in Diamonds, U.S. Jury Told." December 10, 2013. *Financial Post*. https://financialpost.com/legal-post/ex-madoff-programmers-wanted-payment-in-diamonds-a-u-s-jury-heard.

"Former Director of Operations for Bernard L. Madoff Investment Securities, Daniel Bonventre, Sentenced in Manhattan Federal Court to 10 Years in Prison for His Role in the Massive Fraud." December 8, 2014. U.S. Department of Justice, Southern District of New York. www.justice.gov/usao-sdny/pr/former-director-operations-bernard-l-madoff-investment-securities-daniel-bonventre.

"Investigation of Failure of the SEC to Uncover Bernard Madoff's Ponzi Scheme—Public Version." August 31, 2009. *U.S. Securities and Exchange Commission, Office of Investigations, Report No. OIG-509*, pp. 64–65. www.sec.gov/files/oig-509.pdf.

"Madoff Whistleblower: SEC Failed to Do the Math." March 2, 2010. *Morning Edition*. NPR. www.npr.org/templates/story/story.php?storyId=124208012.

"Madoff's Marvelous Returns: We Explore the Investment Returns Behind the World's Largest Ever Ponzi Scheme." April 16, 2017. *Chartr Newsletter*. www.chartr.co/stories/2021-04-16-1-bernie-madoffs-returns.

"The Rise and Fall of Madoff's Ponzi Scheme." April 24, 2021. *Reveal*. https://revealnews.org/podcast/the-rise-and-fall-of-madoffs-ponzi-scheme/.

"Weighing the Value of the Bargain: Prosecutorial Discretion After Sentencing Guidelines." August 2019. *Criminal Justice Policy Review*.

9-47.120—FCPA Corporate Enforcement Policy. 2019. *Credit for Voluntary Self-Disclosure, Full Cooperation, and Timely and Appropriate Remediation in FCPA Matters* at 1. www.justice.gov/criminal-fraud/file/838416/download

April 23, 2018 Letter from the Department of Justice, Criminal Division, Fraud Section to Hogan Lovells, law firm representing The Dun & Bradstreet Corporation. 2021. www.justice.gov/criminal-fraud/file/1055401/download (accessed July 14, 2021).

Armenakis, A.A. September 2002. "Boisjoly on Ethics: An Interview With Roger M. Boisjoly." *Journal of Management Inquiry* 11, p. 277.

Associated Press. December 16, 2007. "Pettitte Admits Using HGH to Recover From Elbow Injury in 2002." *ESPN*. http://sports.espn.go.com/mlb/news/story?id=3156305.

Baily, M.N., R.E. Litan, and M.S. Johnson. November 2008. *The Origin of the Financial Crisis*, p. 8. New York, NY: The Brookings Institute. www.brookings.edu/wp-content/uploads/2016/06/11_origins_crisis_baily_litan.pdf.

Barnes, J.E. September 7, 2001. "P.&G. Said to Agree to Pay Unilever $10 Million in Spying Case." *New York Times.* www.nytimes.com/2001/09/07/business/p-g-said-to-agree-to-pay-unilever-10-million-in-spying-case.html#:~:text=Procter%20%26%20Gamble%20will%20pay%20Unilever,the%20terms%20of%20the%20settlement.

Bellace, J. May 31, 2022. "Is Workplace Loyalty Gone for Good?." *Knowledge at Wharton.* https://knowledge.wharton.upenn.edu/article/is-workplace-loyalty-gone-for-good/.

Belsky, G. June 18, 2012. "Why (Almost) All of Us Cheat and Steal." *Time.* http://business.time.com/2012/06/18/why-almost-all-of-us-cheat-and-steal/.

Bennett, M.W., J.D. Levinson, and K. Hioki. March 2017. "Judging Federal White-Collar Fraud Sentencing: An Empirical Study Revealing the Need for Further Reform." *Iowa Law Review* 102, p. 939.

Bergman, P. n.d. "Formal Discovery: Gathering Evidence for Your Lawsuit." *NOLO Publishing.* www.nolo.com/legal-encyclopedia/formal-discovery-gathering-evidence-lawsuit-29764.html.

*Bernard L. Madoff Pleads Guilty to 11-Count Criminal Information and Is Remanded Into Custody.* March 12, 2009. The FBI, New York Field Office. https://archives.fbi.gov/archives/newyork/press-releases/2009/nyfo031209.htm.

Bindley, K. September 10, 2021. "Workers Want to Do Their Jobs From Anywhere and Keep Their Big-City Salaries; Employers See Remote Work as an Opportunity to Save Money by Cutting Pay; Employees Argue That Their Work Has the Same Value No Matter Where They Do It." *Wall Street Journal.*

Bok, S. 1998. "Whistleblowing and Professional Responsibility." In *Ethical Theory and Business*, eds. T.L. Beauchamp and N.E. Bowie, pp. 261–262. 2nd ed. Englewood Cliffs, NJ: Prentice-Hall.

Borchers, C. February 24, 2022. "Sorry, Bosses: Workers Are Just Not That Into You." *Wall Street Journal.* www.wsj.com/articles/why-workers-not-back-to-office-bosses-11645640418.

Buckingham, M. May–June 2022. "Designing Work That People Love." *Harvard Business Review.* https://hbr.org/2022/05/designing-work-that-people-love.

Bucy, P., E.P. Formby, M.S. Raspanti, and K.E. Rooney. 2008. "Why Did They Do It? The Motive, Mores and Character of White Collar Criminals." *St. John's Law Review* 82, no. 2, p. 401, Spring.

Carino, A., P. Menor, and B. Kaplan. December 2021. "EU Whistleblower Directive: Key Provisions, SOX Comparison and Actions for Business." *DLA Piper.* www.dlapiper.com/en/insights/publications/2021/06/whistleblowing-guide/key-provisions-sox-comparison-actions-for-business.

Carlson, N. August 12, 2013. "New Info Hints at the Real Reason AOL CEO Tim Armstrong Fired an Executive in Front of 1,000 Coworkers." *Business Insider*. www.businessinsider.com/why-tim-armstrong-fired-abel-lenz-2013-8.

Carozza, D. May/June 2009. "Chasing Madoff: An Interview With Harry Markopolos." *Fraud Magazine*. www.fraud-magazine.com/article.aspx?id=313.

Chambers, R. June 7, 2022. "20 Years Later Worldcom Is Still a Watershed Event for Internal Audit." *Auditboard*. www.auditboard.com/blog/20-years-later-worldcom-is-still-a-watershed-event-for-internal-audit/.

Choo, L. July 31, 2023. "People Are Hiring D-List Celebrities to Deliver Their Bad News." *Wall Street Journal*.

Chuchmach, M., R. Esposito, and A. Katersky. July 14, 2009. "Bernie Madoff 'Hit the Inmate Lottery' With Butner Prison, Consultant Says." *ABC News*. https://abcnews.go.com/Blotter/Madoff/story?id=8080354&page=1.

Clifton, J. June 14, 2022. "The World's Workplace Is Broken—Here's How to Fix It." *Gallup Workplace*. www.gallup.com/workplace/393395/world-workplace-broken-fix.aspx.

Clifton, J. June 21, 2023. "Why the World Is Quiet Quitting." *Gallup*. www.gallup.com/workplace/507650/why-world-quit-quiet-quitting.aspx.

Cole, S. n.d. "How to Cultivate Employee Loyalty During Covid-19 and Beyond." https://cowenpartners.com/how-to-cultivate-employee-loyalty-during-covid-19-and-beyond/.

Copeland, M.K. 2014. "The Emerging Significance of Values Based Leadership: A Literature Review." *International Journal of Leadership Studies* 2, no. 8. www.regent.edu/journal/international-journal-of-leadership-studies/significance-of-values-based-leadership/

Criminal Division of the U.S. Department of Justice and the Enforcement Division of the U.S. Securities and Exchange Commission. July 2020. *FCPA—A Resource Guide to the U.S. Foreign Corrupt Practices Act*, p. 51, 58, 71. 2nd ed. www.justice.gov/criminal-fraud/file/1292051/download (accessed July 14, 2021).

Deczynski, R. December 14, 2021. "Workers Keep Resigning. Here's a Novel Idea to Get Them to Stay." *Inc.* www.inc.com/rebecca-deczynski/great-resignation-quitting-stay-interviews.html.

Deloitte. 2015. *Corporate Culture: The Second Ingredient in a World-Class Ethics and Compliance Program*. www2.deloitte.com/content/dam/Deloitte/us/Documents/risk/us-aers-corporate-culture-112514.pdf.

Deloitte. 2021. *The Future of Trust: A New Measure for Enterprise Performance*. www2.deloitte.com/content/dam/Deloitte/us/Documents/risk/future-of-trust-pov-21.pdf.

Department of Health and Human Services: Office of Inspector General. n.d. *Corporate Integrity Agreements*. https://oig.hhs.gov/compliance/corporate-integrity-agreements/index.asp.

Department of Health and Human Services: Office of Inspector General. February 23, 1998. *Publication of the OIG Compliance Program Guidance for Hospitals, No. 35, 63 Fed, Reg.* https://oig.hhs.gov/authorities/docs/cpghosp.pdf.

Department of Justice, Office of Public Affairs. 2018. *Legg Mason Inc. Agrees to Pay $64 Million in Criminal Penalties and Disgorgement to Resolve FCPA Charges Related to Bribery of Gaddafi-Era Libyan Officials.* www.justice.gov/opa/pr/legg-mason-inc-agrees-pay-64-million-criminal-penalties-and-disgorgement-resolve-fcpa-charges (accessed July 23, 2021).

Department of Justice, Office of Public Affairs. October 22, 2020. *Goldman Sachs Charged in Foreign Bribery Case and Agrees to Pay Over $2.9 Billion.* www.justice.gov/opa/pr/goldman-sachs-charged-foreign-bribery-case-and-agrees-pay-over-29-billion (accessed July 20, 2021).

Deputy Attorney General Lisa O. Monaco Delivers Remarks on Corporate Criminal Enforcement. September 15, 2022. www.justice.gov/opa/speech/deputy-attorney-general-lisa-o-monaco-delivers-remarks-corporate-criminal-enforcement.

Deputy Attorney General Lisa O. Monaco Gives Keynote Address at ABA's 36th National Institute on White Collar Crime, Department of Justice News. October 28, 2021. www.justice.gov/opa/speech/deputy-attorney-general-lisa-o-monaco-gives-keynote-address-abas-36th-national-institute.

Detert, J.R. November–December 2018. "Cultivating Everyday Courage." *Harvard Business Review.* https://hbr.org/2018/11/cultivating-everyday-courage.

*Dow Jones.* n.d. "What Are Non-Prosecution Agreements (NPAs) and Deferred Prosecution Agreements (DPAs)?." https://professional.dowjones.com/risk/glossary/anti-bribery-corruption/npa-dpa/.

Dunn, G. January 19, 2021. *2020 Year-End Update on Corporate Non-Prosecution Agreements and Deferred Prosecution Agreements.* www.gibsondunn.com/2020-year-end-update-on-corporate-non-prosecution-agreements-and-deferred-prosecution-agreements/ (accessed July 23, 2021).

Dunn, G. October 1, 2020. *Negotiating Closure of Government Investigations: NPAs, DPAs, and Beyond,* p. 7. www.gibsondunn.com/wp-content/uploads/2020/10/WebcastSlides-Negotiating-Closure-of-Government-Investigations-NPAs-DPAs-and-Beyond-01-OCT-2020.pdf (accessed July 21, 2021).

Edelhertz, H. 1970. *The Nature, Impact, and Prosecution of White Collar Crime,* p. 3. National Institute of Law Enforcement and Criminal Justice. www.ojp.gov/pdffiles1/Digitization/4415NCJRS.pdf.

Egan, M. September 9, 2016. "Workers Tell Wells Fargo Horror Stories." *CNN Business.* https://money.cnn.com/2016/09/09/investing/wells-fargo-phony-accounts-culture/index.html.

Ellis, L. and A. Yang. August 12, 2022. "If Your Co-Workers Are 'Quiet Quitting,' Here's What That Means." *Wall Street Journal.* www.wsj.com/articles/if-your-gen-z-co-workers-are-quiet-quitting-heres-what-that-means-11660260608.

*Ethics Unwrapped.* n.d. "Incrementalism." https://ethicsunwrapped.utexas.edu/glossary/incrementalism.

Ethisphere. January 2020. *Insights From Our Culture Quotient Data Set: Volume Two 7.* https://ethisphere.com/wp-content/uploads/Ethical-Culture-Insights-PartTwo-Jan2020.pdf (accessed May 13, 2021).

Ethisphere. November 2019. *Insights From Our Culture Quotient Data Set: Volume One 4.* Scottsdale. https://ethisphere.com/wp-content/uploads/Ethical-Culture-Insights-PartOne.pdf.

Feintzeig, R. August 13, 2021. "These People Who Work From Home Have a Secret: They Have Two Jobs." *Wall Street Journal.*

Filabi, A. and C. Bulgarella. 2018. "Organizational Culture Drives Ethical Behaviour: Evidence From Pilot Studies." *2018 OECD Global Anti-Corruption & Integrity Forum,* p. 5.

Fishman, S. February 25, 2011. "The Madoff Tapes." New York, NY. https://nymag.com/news/features/berniemadoff-2011-3/.

Flitter, E. February 21, 2020. "The Price of Wells Fargo's Fake Account Scandal Grows by $3 Billion." *New York Times.* www.nytimes.com/2020/02/21/business/wells-fargo-settlement.html.

Frahrenthold, D. August 3, 2014. "For Whistleblowers, a Bold Move Can Be Followed by One to the Department Basement." *The Washington Post.* www.washingtonpost.com/politics/for-whistleblowers-bold-move-can-be-followed-by-one-to-department-basement/2014/08/03/39d12656-182f-11e4-9e3b-7f2f110c6265_story.html?tid=ss_mail.

Gaul, M. November 4, 2013. "The Fraud Triangle." *The Risk Management Blog.* www.lowersriskgroup.com/blog/2013/11/04/fraud-triangle-infographic/.

GE. n.d. *2000 Annual Report 5.* www.annualreports.com/HostedData/AnnualReportArchive/g/NYSE_GE_2000.pdf.

Gerstner, L. 2003. *Who Says Elephants Can't Dance? Leading a Great Enterprise Through Dramatic Change,* pp. 181–182. New York, NY: Harper Collins.

Gibbs, A. April 4, 2022. "Boss Pretending to Fire Employee as April Fools Sparks Backlash Online." *Newsweek.* www.newsweek.com/boss-pretending-fire-employee-april-fools-backlash-online-1694619.

Gibeaut, J. May 2006. "Culture Clash: Other Countries Don't Embrace Sarbanes or America's Reverence of Whistle-Blowers." *A.B.A. Journal.* www.abajournal.com/magazine/article/culture_clash.

Greenleaf, D.E. July 4, 2022. "A Rude Awakening Is Ahead of Young Employees." *Wall Street Journal.*

Groenewald, L. 2022. *The Whistleblowing Non-Retaliation Toolkit*, p. 23. Pretoria, The Ethics Institute. www.tei.org.za/wp-content/uploads/2022/04/Final_-The-Whistleblowing-Non-Retaliation-Toolkit_ISBN-978-0-620-99796-6_ebook.pdf.

Groysberg, B., J. Lee, J. Price, and J.Y.-J. Cheng. January–February 2018. "The Leader's Guide to Corporate Culture." *Harvard Business Review*. https://hbr.org/2018/01/the-leaders-guide-to-corporate-culture.

Harter, J. January 25, 2023. "U.S. Employee Engagement Needs a Rebound in 2023." *Gallup*, p. 2. www.gallup.com/workplace/468233/employee-engagement-needs-rebound-2023.aspx.

Haugh, T. and S. Bedi. n.d. "Valuing Corporate Compliance." *109 Iowa Law Review (Forthcoming)*. https://ssrn.com/abstract=4380918 or http://dx.doi.org/10.2139/ssrn.4380918.

Haugh, T. n.d. "Crime Is a Learned Behavior." (post). *Linkedin*. www.linkedin.com/posts/todd-haugh-811a2137_breaking-outcome-health-execs-convicted-activity-7051600933620772864-bfH1.

Henriksson, K. and J. Stappers. April 7, 2022. "The EU Whistleblowing Directive." *Navex*. www.navex.com/blog/article/the-eu-whistleblowing-directive/.

Henriques, D.B. June 29, 2009. "Madoff Is Sentenced to 150 Years for Ponzi Scheme." *The New York Times*. www.nytimes.com/2009/06/30/business/30madoff.html.

Hickman, A. and J. Pietrocini. May 8, 2019. "How to Help Your Managers Build Out, Not Burn Out." *Gallup Workplace*. www.gallup.com/workplace/249140/inspire-management-breakthrough-not-breakdown.aspx.

Horwitz, J. October 4, 2021. "Whistleblower Says Her Motive Is to Fix Facebook." *Wall Street Journal*.

IMDb Quotes—Page for *Boiler Room*. 2000. "Ben Affleck: Jim Young." www imdb.com/title/tt0181984/characters/nm0000255.

IMDb, *A Few Good Men*. 1991. www.imdb.com/title/tt0104257/quotes/qt1870496.

IMDb—Page for *Office Space*. 1991. "Quotes." https://www.imdb.com/title/tt0151804/quotes/

IMDb—Page for *The Company Men*. 2010. "Chris Cooper: Phil Woodward." www.imdb.com/title/tt1172991/characters/nm0177933.

Internet Movie Database. IMDb—Page for *Office Space*. 1991. "Mike Judge: Chotchkie's Manager." www.imdb.com/title/tt0151804/characters/nm0431918.

Internet Movie Script Database (IMSDb), Page for *A Few Good Men*. 1991. www.imsdb.com/scripts/A-Few-Good-Men.html.

Ito, A. May 22, 2022. "If You've Stayed Put at Your Company During the Great Resignation You're Paying a Price for Your Loyalty." *Business Insider*. www.businessinsider.com/great-resignation-pay-gap-new-hires-earning-more-2022-5.

Jennings, M. 2018. "The Moving Line." *Business Ethics: Case Studies and Selected Readings*, p. 192. 9th ed. Boston: Cengage.

Judge Denny Chin, Sentencing Bernard L. Madoff, Statement by Judge Denny Chin, (p. 49 lines 14–22) 96TJMADF, 09 CR 213 (DC). June 29, 2009. www.justice.gov/usao-sdny/file/762821/download.

Kanter, R.M. and M. Bird. September 2009. *Procter & Gamble in the 21st Century (A): Becoming Truly Global*. Harvard Business Publishing.

Keeley, M. June 15, 2022. "'Never Find Work': Recruiter Mocked for Anger at Prospect's Current Salary." *Newsweek*. https://worldtimetodays.com/recruiter-mocked-for-anger-at-prospects-current-salary/.

Kelly, A. December 12, 2017. "James Burke: The Johnson & Johnson CEO Who Earned a Presidential Medal of Freedom." www.jnj.com/our-heritage/james-burke-johnson-johnson-ceo-who-earned-presidential-medal-of-freedom.

Keneally, K. 2004. "Corporate Compliance Programs: From the Sentencing Guidelines to the Thompson Memorandum and Back Again." *Champion*, p. 46.

Kenvue. n.d. "Our Values." www.kenvue.com/our-story.

Kimes, M. August 19, 2010. "Why J&J's Headache Won't Go Away." *Fortune*.

Knight, J. October 11, 1982. "Tylenol's Maker Shows How to Respond to a Crisis." *The Washington Post*. www.washingtonpost.com/archive/business/1982/10/11/tylenols-maker-shows-how-to-respond-to-crisis/bc8df898-3fcf-443f-bc2f-e6fbd639a5a3/.

Koehler, M. April 4, 2013. *Former Attorney General Alberto Gonzales Criticizes Various Aspects of DOJ FCPA Enforcment*. FCPA Professor. https://fcpaprofessor.com/former-attorney-general-alberto-gonzales-criticizes-various-aspects-of-doj-fcpa-enforcement/ (accessed July 22, 2021).

Koehler, M. 2015. "Measuring the Impact of Non-Prosecution and Deferred Prosecution Agreements on Foreign Corrupt Practices Act Enforcement, 49." *University of California Davis Law Review* 497, p. 502, 522.

Koppel, T. June 14, 1998. "Commencement Address to Stanford University." www.101bananas.com/library2/koppel.html.

*L'Oréal Code of Ethics: The Way We Work*. n.d. p. 8. 3rd ed. Paris: SVP and Chief Ethics Officer L'Oréal.

Larmer, R.A. 1992. "Whistleblowing and Employee Loyalty." *Journal of Business Ethics* 11, p. 126, 127.

Lefcoe, G. December 18, 1998. "Notable & Quotable." *Wall Street Journal*, A14. Eastern Edition.

Liu, J. November 3, 2021. "Why All Your Coworkers Who Quit Are About to Come Back as 'Boomerang Employees.'" *CNBC*. www.cnbc.com/2021/11/03/great-resignation-could-fuel-the-rise-of-the-boomerang-employee.html.

Lufkin, B. June 30, 2022. "'Zoom Firing': Are Virtual Layoffs the Future?." *Worklife*. www.bbc.com/worklife/article/20220630-zoom-firing-are-virtual-layoffs-the-future.

MacFarquhar, L. May 14, 2012. "When Giants Fail: What Business Has Learned From Clayton Christensen." *The New Yorker*.

Mangan, D. July 23, 2021. "Ponzi Schemer Madoff Earned $710 for Almost 3,000 Hours of Prison Work, Got 'Not Very Dependable' Review." *CNBC*. www.cnbc.com/2021/07/23/bernie-madoff-earned-710-in-prison-after-ponzi-fraud-conviction.html.

Mark, G. January 19, 2017. "Bernie Madoff Is Cornering the Hot Chocolate Market—in Prison." *Washington Post*. www.washingtonpost.com/news/on-small-business/wp/2017/01/19/bernie-madoff-is-cornering-the-hot-chocolate-market-in-prison/.

Marks, G. March 20, 2022. "Turns Out the Great Resignation May Be Followed by the Great Regret." *The Guardian*. www.theguardian.com/business/2022/mar/20/great-resignation-great-regret-employees-quitting.

Marks, J. November 2012. "A Matter of Ethics: Understanding the Mind of a White-Collar Criminal." *Financial Executive* 28, p. 33.

Maruf, R. December 6, 2021. "Better.com CEO Fires 900 Employees Over Zoom." *CNN Business*. www.cnn.com/2021/12/05/business/better-ceo-fires-employees.

Mathiason, G.G. and A.D. Weindling. December 2005. "Toward the End of the French Exception?: Overcoming the Challenges of Establishing a Global 'Whistleblower' Hotline." *Littler Mendelson Time Sensitive Newsletter*. www.littler.com/files/press/pdf/13130.pdf.

Mauro, T. January 13, 2005. "Federal Sentencing Guidelines Ordered Relegated to Advisory Role by High Court." *The Legal Intelligencer*.

Mayer, R.C., J.H. Davis, and F.D. Schoorman. 1995. "An Integrative Model of Organizational Trust." *Academy of Management Review* 20, no. 3, pp. 709–734.

McClennan, M. March 11, 2019. "What Do the World's Most Ethical Companies Have in Common: Ethisphere's Erica Salmon Byrne Answers That Question." *Ethical Voices*. www.ethicalvoices.com/2019/03/11/what-the-worlds-most-ethical-companies-have-in-common-ethispheres-erica-salmon-byrne/.

McLain, D. and R. Pendell. April 17, 2023. "Why Trust in Leaders Is Faltering and How to Gain It Back." www.gallup.com/workplace/473738/why-trust-leaders-faltering-gain-back.aspx.

Memorandum by Sally Quillian Yates. September 9, 2015. "Individual Accountability for Corporate Wrongdoing." *U.S. Department of Justice*, p. 3. www.justice.gov/archives/dag/file/769036/download.

Memorandum from Mark Filip, Deputy Att'y Gen. August 28, 2008. *U.S. Dep't of Justice, to the Heads of Dep't Components, U.S. Attorneys*, p. 18. www.justice.gov/sites/default/files/dag/legacy/2008/11/03/dag-memo-08282008.pdf.

Milgram, S. 1974. *Obedience to Authority: An Experimental View*, p. 4. New York, NY: Harper Collins.

Millman, G.J. October 24, 2013. "Q&A: Dan Roach, Vice President Compliance and Audit, Dignity Health." *Wall Street Journal*. www.wsj.com/articles/BL-252B-2784.

Moberly, R.E. October 2007. "Unfulfilled Expectations: An Empirical Analysis of Why Sarbanes-Oxley Whistleblowers Rarely Win." *William and Mary law review* 49, p. 67.

Molla, R. January 11, 2022. "American Workers Have Power. That Won't Last Forever." *Vox.* www.vox.com/recode/22841490/work-remote-wages-labor-force-participation-great-resignation-unions-quits.

Molla, R. May 30, 2022. "Tell Your Boss: Working From Home Is Making You More Productive." *Vox.* www.vox.com/recode/23129752/work-from-home-productivity.

Morgenson, G. February 19, 2011. "How a Whistle-Blower Conquered Countrywide." *New York Times.* www.nytimes.com/2011/02/20/business/20gret.html?pagewanted=1&_r=1&adxnnl=1&ref=business&adxnnlx=1298149225-m4UqeuczpZ9OWTl9IkD%204g.

Near, J.P. and P. Miceli. 1985. "Organizational Dissidence: The Case of Whistle-Blowing." *Journal of Business Ethics* 4, p. 10.

Nguyen, T. April 22, 2022. "Gen Z Does Not Dream of Labor." *Vox.* www.vox.com/the-highlight/22977663/gen-z-antiwork-capitalism.

Nisen, M. November 22, 2013. "Tony Hsieh's Brilliant Strategy for Hiring Kind People." *Insider.* www.businessinsider.com/tony-hsieh-zappos-hiring-strategy-2013-11.

NPR. June 4, 2012. "The 'Truth' About Why We Lie, Cheat and Steal." *All Things Considered.* www.npr.org/2012/06/04/154287476/honest-truth-about-why-we-lie-cheat-and-steal.

Oliver, S. November 26, 2021. "How to Build Stronger Relationships With Colleagues in the Zoom Era; Research Shows That Colleagues Who Work Remotely Can Develop the Same Levels of Trust as Those Working Face-to-Face. It Just Takes Longer." *Wall Street Journal.*

Olson, S.D. 2013. *SHRM Foundation's Effective Practice Guidelines Series: Shaping an Ethical Workplace Culture*, p. 6, 13, 15, 18. Briggs and Morgan, P.A., The Kenrich Group LLC.

Otto.Law. February 10, 2020. "The Question of White Collar Crime and Jail Time." www.otto.law/blog/2020/02/the-question-of-white-collar-crime-and-jail-time/.

Parsi, N. March 25, 2022. "6 Strategies for Building Employee Loyalty." *SHRM.*

Pearlstein, J. June 22, 2021. "Why We Lie, Go to Prison and Eat Cake: 10 Questions With Dan Ariely." *Wired.* www.wired.com/2012/06/why-we-lie-cheat-go-to-prison-and-eat-chocolate-cake-10-questions-with-dan-ariely/.

Pendell, R. June 14, 2022. "Fixing The World's $7.8 Trillion Workplace Problem." *Gallup Workplace.* www.gallup.com/workplace/393497/world-trillion-workplace-problem.aspx#:~:text=Employees%20who%20are%20not%20engaged,employees%20were%20engaged%20at%20work.

Pepper, J. 2005. *What Really Matters, The Procter & Gamble Company*, p. 246. Cincinnati, Ohio: One Procter & Gamble Plaza.

Peterson, J. March–April 2020. "Firing With Compassion." *Harvard Business Review.* https://hbr.org/2020/03/firing-with-compassion.

Prager, J. 2013. "The Financial Crisis of 2007/8: Misaligned Incentives, Bank Mismanagement, and Troubling Policy Implications." *Economics, Management, and Financial Markets* 8, no. 2, p. 25.

Prentice, R.A. 2015. "Behavioral Ethics: Can It Help Lawyers (and Others) Be Their Best Selves." *Notre Dame Journal of Law, Ethics & Public Policy* 29, no. 1, pp. 52–53, 57.

Ramirez, M.K. 2019. "Whistling Past the Graveyard: Dodd-Frank Whistleblower Programs Dodge Bullets Fighting Financial Crime." *Loyola University Chicago Law Journal* 50, p. 620, Spring.

Reimann, N. April 14, 2021. "Bernie Madoff Dies in Federal Prison at 82." *Forbes.* www.forbes.com/sites/nicholasreimann/2021/04/14/bernie-madoff-dies-in-federal-prison-at-82/?sh=183f42a3fadd.

Riley, C. and R. Iyengar. May 11, 2018. "Whistleblower 'Mistakes' Cost Barclays CEO $1.5 Million." *CNN Business.* https://money.cnn.com/2018/05/11/investing/barclays-ceo-jes-staley-fine-pay/index.html.

Ripley, A. December 30, 2002. "Cynthia Cooper: The Night Detective." *Time.* https://content.time.com/time/subscriber/article/0,33009,1003990,00.html

Rowland, T. February 8, 2020. "Congress Protected Whistleblowers During American Revolution." *The Herald-Mail (Hagerstown, Maryland).*

S. Rep. No. 107-146, at 10. 2002. www.congress.gov/congressional-report/107th-congress/senate-report/146/1.

Samuel, A. September 24, 2020. "Remote Work: How to Build and Maintain an Office Culture Without an Office; Working From Home Makes It Hard to Create Norms That Every Employee Knows to Follow. But There Are Ways to Do It." *Wall Street Journal.*

Sandburg, C. 1954. *Abraham Lincoln: The Prairie Years and the War Years*, p. 278. New York, NY: Harcourt Brace Jovanovich.

Sandford, N. January 19, 2018. "Corporate Culture: The Center of Strong Ethics and Compliance." *Wall Street Journal.* https://deloitte.wsj.com/articles/corporate-culture-the-center-of-strong-ethics-and-compliance-1516338129.

Savage, D. August 3, 2004. "Federal sentencing guidelines." Interview by Neal Conan. *Talk of the Nation*. NPR.

Schatz, J. January 7, 2014, Updated 17, 2022. "5 Ways to Increase Employee Engagement." *Workplace Gallup*. www.gallup.com/workplace/231581/five-ways-improve-employee-engagement.aspx.

Schulmann, R. 2014. "Einstein's Politics." In *The Cambridge Companion to Einstein*, eds. M. Janssen and C. Lehner, p. 426. Cambridge, UK: Cambridge University Press.

Schulweis, R.H.M. 2010. *Conscience: The Duty to Obey and the Duty to Disobey*, p. 106. Woodstock, VT: Longhill Partners.

Schwartz, M. May 22, 2018. "Warren Buffett Says If You Hire Somebody Without This Trait, 'You Really Want Them to Be Dumb and Lazy." *Inc.*

Scudamore, B. October 5, 2016. "How to Create Awesome Workplace Culture With Storytelling." *Forbes*. www.forbes.com/sites/brianscudamore/2016/10/05/how-to-create-awesome-workplace-culture-with-storytelling/?sh=282bfca228d5.

Segal, E. October 5, 2021. "The Great Disconnect: Many More Employers Than Workers Want to Return to Offices." *Forbes*. www.forbes.com/sites/edwardsegal/2021/10/05/the-great-disconnect-many-more-employers-than-workers-want-to-return-to-offices/?sh=fe995d51ad3d.

Sherman, A. and S. Whitten. January 9, 2023. "Bob Iger Tells Disney Employees They Must Return to the Office Four Days a Week." *CNBC*. www.cnbc.com/2023/01/09/disney-ceo-bob-iger-tells-employees-to-return-to-the-office-four-days-a-week.html.

Smith, G., Op-ed Contributor. March 14, 2012. "Why I Am Leaving Goldman Sachs." *New York Times*. www.nytimes.com/2012/03/14/opinion/why-i-am-leaving-goldman-sachs.html.

Southern, K. August 1, 2023. "Celebrities Paid to Be Bearers of Bad News." *The Times*. www.thetimes.co.uk/article/celebrities-paid-to-be-bearers-of-bad-news-f9ps0st7g.

Stappers, J. April 19, 2022. "EU Whistleblower Directive: Addressing Differences in Country Transposition." *WhistleB, A Navex Company*. https://www.navexglobal.com/blog/article/eu-whistleblower-directive-addressing-differences-in-country-transposition/?source=JD%20Supra.

Storbeck, O. June 7, 2023. "Markus Braun Told Wirecard's Top Lawyer That Compliance Was 'Crap', Court Hears." *Financial Times*. www.ft.com/content/ab127025-1eb2-49bb-9437-4af86c943103.

Sutherland, E.H. 1949. *White Collar Crime*, p. 9. New York, NY: Dryden Press.

Tedlow, R.S. and W.K. Smith. October 20, 2005. "James Burke: A Career in American Business (B)." *Harvard Business School*, p. 3.

Terkel, S. 1974. *Working*, p. 405. New York, NY: The New Press.

*Testimony December 14, 1995 Richard P. Conaboy Chairman United States Sentencing Commission House Judiciary Crime Sentencing Commission, Federal Document Clearing House Congressional Testimony.* December 14, 1995.

*The Financial Express.* August 11, 2010. "FE Editorial: Protecting whistleblowers." www.financialexpress.com/archive/fe-editorial-protecting-whistleblowers/658669/.

The Internet Movie Database. IMDb's Page for *Snake Eyes*. 1998. "Snake Eyes Quotes." www.imdb.com/title/tt0120832/quotes.

Thielman, S. January 12, 2017. "Never-Before-Heard Bernie Madoff Tapes Reveal Details of Ruinous Ponzi Scheme." *The Guardian.* www.theguardian.com/business/2017/jan/12/bernie-madoff-prison-life-ponzi-supernova-podcast-experience.

Thornton, G. March 28, 2019. "Culture Payoff: Looking for ROI in All the Right Places." www.grantthornton.com/library/articles/advisory/2019/return-on-culture/looking-ROI-in-all-right-places.aspx.

Treviño, L.K., G.R. Weaver, D.G. Gibson, and B.L. Toffler. 1999. "Managing Ethics and Legal Compliance: What Works and What Hurts." *California Management Review* 41, no. 2, pp. 141–142, 143, 145,Winter.

Tsipursky, G. August 1, 2023. "We're Now Finding Out the Damaging Results of the Mandated Return to the Office—and It's Worse Than We Thought." *Fortune.*

Tsipursky, G. November 3, 2022. "Workers Are Less Productive Working Remotely (At Least That's What Their Bosses Think)." *Forbes.* www.forbes.com/sites/glebtsipursky/2022/11/03/workers-are-less-productive-working-remotely-at-least-thats-what-their-bosses-think/?sh=33112a6a286a.

Twitter. May 9, 2022. 9:20AM. @elonmusk. https://twitter.com/elonmusk/status/1523654106745020418?lang=en.

U.S. Department of Justice Criminal Division: Evaluation of Corporate Compliance Programs. Updated June 2020. pp. 1–2. www.justice.gov/criminal-fraud/page/file/937501/download.

U.S. Department of Justice Criminal Division: Evaluation of Corporate Compliance Programs. Updated March 2023. p. 9. www.justice.gov/criminal-fraud/page/file/937501/download.

U.S. Securities and Exchange Commission (Press Release). September 15, 2021. *SEC Surpasses $1 Billion in Awards to Whistleblower With Two Awards Totaling $114 Million.* www.sec.gov/news/press-release/2021-177.

U.S. Securities and Exchange Commission. September 23, 2020. *SEC Adds Clarity, Efficiency and Transparency to Its Successful Whistleblower Award Program.* www.sec.gov/news/press-release/2020-219.

United States of America v. Bernard L. Madoff, Sentencing by Judge Denny Chin, 96TJMADF, 09 CR 213 (DC). June 29, 2009. pp. 47–48. www.justice.gov/usao-sdny/file/762821/download.

Used with permission from Procter & Gamble. n.d. https://us.pg.com/policies-and-practices/purpose-values-and-principles/.

Vance, S.E. January 2019. "Weighing the Value of the Bargain: Prosecutorial Discretion After Sentencing Guidelines." *Criminal Justice Policy Review* 30, no. 7.

Vozza, S. January 5, 2002. "This CEO Pays New Employees $5,000 to Quit." *Fast Company.* www.fastcompany.com/90708440/this-ceo-pays-new-employees-5000-to-quit.

Walker, B. and S.A. Soule. June 20, 2017. "Changing Company Culture Requires a Movement, Not a Mandate." *Harvard Business Review.* https://hbr.org/2017/06/changing-company-culture-requires-a-movement-not-a-mandate.

Warren Buffett to Berkshire Hathaway Managers, Memorandum. October 9, 2006. *Financial Times.* www.ft.com/content/48312832-57d4-11db-be9f-0000779e2340.

Wayne, L. September 3, 2012. "Foreign Firms Most Affected by U.S. Law Barring Bribes." *New York Times.* www.nytimes.com/2012/09/04/business/global/bribery-settlements-under-us-law-are-mostly-with-foreign-countries.html?pagewanted=all&_r=0 (accessed July 23, 2021).

Weiser, B. June 28, 2011. "Judge Explains 150-Year Sentence for Madoff." *The New York Times.* www.nytimes.com/2011/06/29/nyregion/judge-denny-chin-recounts-his-thoughts-in-bernard-madoff-sentencing.html.

Woodford, M. 2014. *Exposure: Inside the Olympus Scandal: How I Went From CEO to Whistleblower*, p. 111. New York, NY: Portfolio/Penguin.

Zappos. n.d. *What We Live By: Our Core Values.* www.zappos.com/about/what-we-live-by

Zetter, K. November 13, 2009. "Madoff's Coders Charged With Aiding Massive Ponzi Scheme." *Wired.* www.wired.com/2009/11/madoff-programmers/.

# About the Author

**Paul Fiorelli** is the Director of the Cintas Institute for Business Ethics at Xavier University. He was selected as a Supreme Court Fellow assigned to the United States Sentencing Commission. During his fellowship year, he received the "Thomas Clark Fellow Award" from Chief Justice Rehnquist. Fiorelli was also honored with the 2007 International Compliance Award from the Society of Corporate Compliance and Ethics.

Fiorelli received both his law and MBA degrees and is a tenured Professor at Xavier University. He also teaches a course on Ethics and Compliance at CY Cergy Paris University Law School. At Xavier, he's received numerous teaching awards, including the 2023 MBA Professor of the Year. Fiorelli actively presents to Fortune 500 companies, universities, professional associations, and government agencies.

# Index

## OTHER TITLES IN THE BUSINESS ETHICS AND CORPORATE CITIZENSHIP COLLECTION

Michael J. Provitera and Michael Edmondson, Editors

- *Conscious Business Ethics* by Wade M. Chumney
- *Managing Abundance* by Pradeep Nevatia and Rahul Nevatia
- *Transforming Towards Life-Centered Economies* by Sandra Waddock
- *Grappling With The Gray* by Yonason Goldson
- *Business Ethics and Rational Corporate Policies* by Konstantinos Mantzaris
- *Business and the Culture of Ethics* by Quentin Langley
- *Corporate Citizenship and Sustainability* by Jayaraman Rajah Iyer
- *Applied Humanism* by Jennifer Hancock
- *Powerful Performance* by Mark Eyre
- *Educating Business Professionals* by Lana S. Nino and Susan D. Gotsch
- *Adapting to Change* by Ann Goodman
- *Social Media Ethics Made Easy* by Joseph W. Barnes
- *War Stories* by Leigh Hafrey
- *Shaping the Future of Work* by Thomas A. Kochan
- *Working Ethically in Finance* by Anthony Asher

## Concise and Applied Business Books

The Collection listed above is one of 30 business subject collections that Business Expert Press has grown to make BEP a premiere publisher of print and digital books. Our concise and applied books are for...

- Professionals and Practitioners
- Faculty who adopt our books for courses
- Librarians who know that BEP's Digital Libraries are a unique way to offer students ebooks to download, not restricted with any digital rights management
- Executive Training Course Leaders
- Business Seminar Organizers

Business Expert Press books are for anyone who needs to dig deeper on business ideas, goals, and solutions to everyday problems. Whether one print book, one ebook, or buying a digital library of 110 ebooks, we remain the affordable and smart way to be business smart. For more information, please visit www.businessexpertpress.com, or contact sales@businessexpertpress.com.

Printed in the USA
CPSIA information can be obtained
at www.ICGtesting.com
CBHW072126310324
6099CB00003B/6